A LAP OF AUSTRALIA FOR BEGINNERS

MAY B WILD

© May B Wild 2024

ISBN: 978-1-923163-68-3

 A catalogue record for this book is available from the National Library of Australia

Published by Clark & Mackay, Brisbane QLD Australia
All rights reserved

Although the publisher and the author have made every effort to ensure that the information in this book was correct at press time, and while this publication is designed to provide accurate information in regard to the subject matter covered, the publisher and the author assume no responsibility for errors, inaccuracies, omissions or any other inconsistencies herein and hereby disclaim any liability to any party for any loss, damage or disruption caused by errors or omissions, whether such errors or omissions result from negligence, accident or any other cause.

All hyperlinks in this book were correct at time of print.

It is not legal to reproduce, duplicate or transmit any part of this document in either electronic means or printed format. Recording of this publication is strictly prohibited.

This book is dedicated to my father Rosaire. He was a hard-working, wise and kind man. He also loved to read and would be so proud to know I have written a book. He will be forever travelling with me in my heart.

CONTENTS

Preface ix
Introduction xiii

Part 1 - The Practical Journey 1
Chapter 1
   Whose idea was it anyway? 3
Chapter 2
   What kind of rig do you have? 7
Chapter 3
   Why is it taking so long to go? 13
Chapter 4
   Did you have mobile reception? 17
Chapter 5
   How did you handle the house chores? 21
Chapter 6
   How did you go with the dog? 27
Chapter 7
   What was the weather like? 31
Chapter 8
   Where did you stay at night? 35
Chapter 9
   What does off-road mean anyway? 43
Chapter 10
   What are we doing tonight? 47
Chapter 11
   Did anything scary happen? 51

Chapter 12
Why do we keep getting injured? 57
Chapter 13
How did that break? 61
Chapter 14
How much did it cost? 65

Part 2 - The Magical Journey 73
Chapter 15
Where are we going? 75
Chapter 16
Did you see that? 79
Chapter 17
How many stars are there? 95
Chapter 18
Did you meet anyone interesting? 99
Chapter 19
How weird was that? 111
Chapter 20
Is that another national park? 117
Chapter 21
Is that really art? 131
Chapter 22
How did we miss that? 149

Part 3 - The Educational Journey 155
Chapter 23
Does history repeat? 157
Chapter 24
How fearless were they? 167
Chapter 25
Who invented that? 175
Chapter 26
Is that a gun in your pocket? 181
Chapter 27
Where did they come from? 187

Chapter 28
War: What is it good for?... *191*
Chapter 29
What were they thinking?... *197*
Chapter 30
Is our history black and white?... *205*
Chapter 31
Do you mine?... *215*
Chapter 32
Are diamonds a girl's best friend? *223*
Chapter 33
Who had that bright idea?.. *227*
Chapter 34
How big are the farms? *231*
Chapter 35
Anyone for a glass of wine?.. *237*
Chapter 36
Is it a pub or a hotel?... *245*
Chapter 37
Isn't that beautiful? *251*
Chapter 38
Does it bite?.. *255*

Part 4 - The Emotional Journey 267
Chapter 39
How did your couple survive?... *269*
Chapter 40
Is blood thicker than water?... *273*
Chapter 41
How does it feel to be back home? *277*
A final word 281
Acknowledgements...283
About the author 285

PREFACE

HAVE YOU EVER WANTED TO just get away from it all? And you thought maybe going around Australia was a good idea? The lap of Australia is either a rite of passage or a pipe dream for many Australians.

There are countless ways to travel around Australia. You can go in a circular motion clockwise or anti-clockwise. Another favoured pattern is the figure 8, going through the centre of the country twice. We did not pursue any of those routes and did it *our* way–myself, my husband Chris and our dog Watson. You could say we followed our noses.

We left Brisbane on the 14th of July 2022 and drove for 33,280 kilometres in 326 days. Compare that to driving on National Highway 1 all around Australia, a total distance of 14,500 kilometres. We saw a lot of Australia, yet we are aware that we hardly touched the sides. When people ask us 'What were your favourite places?' we are always stumped for an answer. There were plenty of highlights along the way without a doubt. But it is the *whole* journey that is our favourite without breaking it into smaller parts. It was the adventure of a lifetime.

I migrated from Montreal, Canada to Australia in 1985. After 37 years in my adopted country, I thought I knew Australia. I had visited all the states and lived in three of them. But I was fooling myself and soon found out that I hardly knew anything at all. We learned so much on that road trip about our country and its many facets. We learned a lot more about ourselves and each other.

I kept a daily travel log, which I shared on a private Facebook group for family and friends. I needed to make sure I would not forget the small stuff. I also wanted to share the trip with others who could never entertain such an expedition for whatever reason. There is nothing wrong with armchair travelling and virtual journeys with live videos. People told me they really enjoyed coming along for the ride and miss the daily updates.

This book was born out of a desire to review the whole adventure and cement the learning. And it is a response to the many questions asked of us as to how we did it and what advice we would give to others considering the same.

When we started to plan our journey, we had to answer many questions of the type: 'what', 'when' and 'how'. We had an ever-growing to-do list and dutifully ticked off items as we progressed towards the final goal. It was only when we returned home that the enormity of what we had done dawned on us. We finally asked ourselves, 'Why did we embark on such a wild journey?' We could not possibly have known at the beginning the answers to that question. We just had an urge to go, an itch to scratch! But we do know now, and this book will explain.

KEY

NP: National Park
NSW: New South Wales
NT: Northern Territory
QLD: Queensland
SA: South Australia
VIC: Victoria
WA: Western Australia

*"To move, to breathe, to fly, to float; to gain all while you give;
to roam the roads of lands remote. To travel is to live."*
— Hans Christian Andersen

INTRODUCTION

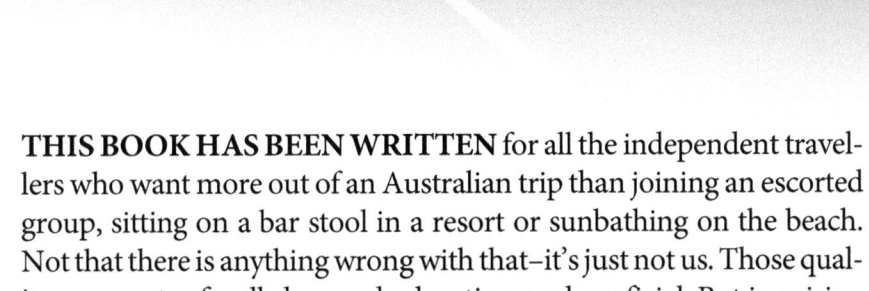

THIS BOOK HAS BEEN WRITTEN for all the independent travellers who want more out of an Australian trip than joining an escorted group, sitting on a bar stool in a resort or sunbathing on the beach. Not that there is anything wrong with that–it's just not us. Those quality moments of well-deserved relaxation are beneficial. But inquiring minds like ours need more stimulation even on holidays.

This is a guide for adults of all ages, including grey nomads, who are planning to go around Australia for a lengthy period of time. It is also recommended reading for armchair travellers who would love to make such a trip but unfortunately cannot. Many people live vicariously!

I have divided the book into distinct journeys rather than a chronological account, to make it easier to categorise all the experiences we encountered. Four components of the trip emerged: *The Practical Journey, The Magical Journey, The Educational Journey* and *The Emotional Journey*.

Each chapter starts with a question that is answered with anecdotes and facts collected over almost one year of travelling. They are questions we asked ourselves or people asked us. I cover the preparation required to find the right mode of transport for your needs, the possible itinerary, and the pitfalls and the glory of achieving such an epic journey through one of the greatest countries on Earth.

Hopefully, you will find the answers entertaining and informative. Ideally, it might set you on your own journey to find out more for yourself. Who knows? You may be inspired to pack up your belongings to travel to the remote areas of Australia sooner than you thought.

"People don't take trips... trips take people."
—*John Steinbeck*

PART 1
The Practical Journey

This section of the book addresses all the logistics of going on such a long road trip as a lap of Australia. It is a complicated process when it is your first time. We really did not know what we were doing. We were absolute beginners. It can be discouraging and easy to give up. Abandoning the dream was never an option, but we came close to it a few times. We looked at many videos of van life influencers. I read many 'Lap of Australia' blogs on the internet and borrowed books from the library. In the end, instinct kicked in and we found our way out of the maze of preparation and on to the wide-open road. Phew and hallelujah!

CHAPTER 1

Whose idea was it anyway?

MY HUSBAND CHRIS AND I both had the idea to travel far and wide. But it did not just happen as a lightbulb moment. Many factors led to the decision to rent out our house for one year and take off into the wilderness. Chris had had a few health scares and COVID-19 brought on his sudden retirement. He was an academic and overseas students stopped coming to Australian universities. Consequently, there was a huge reduction in teaching staff.

My career as an occupational therapist also came to an abrupt and painful stop in 2021 due to workplace bullying. Suddenly I was retired at 60, 10 years earlier than planned. These changes had us rethinking our priorities, like so many during COVID-19, and asking ourselves, 'What is life all about?'

Then Russia invaded Ukraine. Everything seemed so uncertain worldwide. It all looked like doom and gloom. We needed cheering up! We concluded that we should enjoy our golden years while we could, and that would mean only one thing: travel.

We are both seasoned travellers. Chris has been riding motorcycles for 50 years and loves to go bush camping. Each of us has done plenty of international trips. I went around the world

3 times when buying a round-the-world fare was cheaper than a return trip to Montreal!

We were still in the throes of COVID travel restrictions even though they were loosening. So, it was obvious that the best thing to do was the 'lap of Australia' like so many grey nomads. But how do you start preparing for such an event?

I joined a few Facebook groups such as Nomads of Australia, Travel Australia with Dogs and such. I gathered a lot of information about places to look at, tricks and tips about van life, and all the different vehicles available. (The next chapter will deal with the type of rig we decided on.)

But who to rent our Brisbane home to? When we looked at the cost to store all our belongings–and the inconvenience of packing up a 4-bedroom house–we decided to rent the house fully furnished. We offered a mate's rate to our lovely friends Doug and Jan who had done house sitting for us in the past. We knew we could trust them. They paid reduced rent and we got good tenants. We also only had to pack up our personal belongings and store them in the garage. It was a win/win situation.

We fixed our departure date as the first of June 2022. Since we live in Brisbane, it was logical to travel north towards the tropics in winter when it is not so hot. That date kept being moved due to a variety of unforeseen events. (Chapter 3 will delve further into those.)

Are we crazy to go away for so long and so far?

We planned a party to say goodbye to our friends and relatives. Leaving them all behind was a big thing and not done lightly. Our hearts were torn. But we reassured ourselves that we could easily stay in touch with everyone via modern technology. That was wishful thinking. Meanwhile, the farewell gathering of our nearest and dearest at a Brisbane brewery on a sunny Sunday afternoon was absolutely delightful.

But second thoughts slowly started creeping in. *Are we crazy to go away for so long and so far?*

We were committed by then. There was no turning back.

TIPS

Join travel Facebook groups for inspiration such as these two:
https://www.facebook.com/groups/NomadsOfAustraliaTheBestBits
Travel Australia with Dogs: https://www.facebook.com/groups/496641167356061

CHAPTER 2

What kind of rig do you have?

A BIG DECISION TO MAKE was how we were going to travel and thus where we would sleep. That is called a rig. There are literally thousands of different rigs out there and the choice is mind-boggling, from tents, roof top options, camper trailers, fifth wheel trailers, slide-on trailers, purpose-built go-anywhere trucks, standard motorhomes and converted buses of different sizes. We even saw a converted fire truck! It's enough to make your head spin when you start looking into it. We visited a few camping and caravanning shows to get ideas.

What I did know was that camping in a tent was out. There was no way I was going to crawl in and out as my knees would never forgive me. Those days are long gone. Another thing we knew for sure is that we did not want to tow anything. We have a multi-purpose small box trailer we use to tow our kayaks, take rubbish to the tip or transport a motorcycle. We did not even want to tow that. We longed to be free to go wherever without too many hassles. That eliminated all the trailers. Chris wanted a big 'Tonka toy' such as an Oka or Unimog (military type trucks), which are definitely go-anywhere vehicles, but they were out of our budget. Neither could we afford to buy or run a true 4WD motorhome. We needed a rig that could go places with a good ground clearance.

The wish list was:

- self-contained vehicle with shower and toilet
- north-south island double bed (along the van's length)
- full-size fridge/freezer
- off grid capacity with a solar system
- proper trunk (not barn doors out the back)
- low kilometres (less than 150,000 kilometres)
- headroom for 6-foot-tall Chris
- air conditioning
- plenty of drinking water/ black and grey water capacity.

After more research, we figured that a converted Toyota Coaster could possibly tick all our boxes. We looked at Facebook Marketplace for a good deal. Most Coasters for sale are Japanese imports that were used as public transport buses until they clocked 100,000 kilometres. Then they get sold overseas. Australians love those 22 seaters buses as they are rugged enough for our harsh terrain. Some companies specialise in importing them and converting them to motorhomes.

We found a 20-year-old golden Coaster in Bundaberg (QLD) and organised a viewing. We made a day trip out of it as it was nearly 400 kilometres away. It was love at first sight. In hindsight, we were naïve and easily impressed. It was the most expensive Coaster for sale at the time. It had a full-service record for the previous four years (since conversion) and a pile of receipts to prove that it had been well cared for. It all amounted to a lot of money, but we figured it was worth it. A pre-purchase inspection by a local mechanic confirmed that it was mechanically sound. So, we proceeded with the purchase.

The next step was us both getting our Light Rigid (LR) driving license since the bus weighs 5.3 tonnes and is 7.2 metres long. Anything weighing over 4.5 tonnes in Queensland requires that the driver has at least an LR licence. We enrolled and passed the 4-hour course within the next two weeks. We then took the train back to Bundaberg to finalise the sale and take possession of our new home on wheels. We stayed at the local caravan park as it was too late to get on the road at that stage.

A massive thunderstorm hit the region that night. We were relieved to find out that the bus did not leak, and we fell asleep feeling tired but happy. During the night, the wind picked up dramatically and howling sounds all around us kept me awake. Chris is a heavy sleeper. I heard a regular loud clap and thought that a panel on a roof nearby had come loose. However, in the morning light, everything became clear when the sunlight shone through the front of the bus. The loud clapping sound had been our side door banging in the wind. It had not been latched properly and it was wide open. Our poor neighbours must have cursed us! The floor was flooded as the rain had poured in. It was terribly embarrassing to discover our pathetic door locking attempt. It was the first of many mistakes to follow. But some events were to be totally out of our control and nothing to do with our ignorance.

We set off towards home, seriously driving the bus for the first time on highways. It was going relatively well until we smelled smoke. Then the fire alarm went off. We turned in our seats to find the cabin filled with smoke. We had a fire onboard!

> **Here we were, in less than 24 hours of ownership, with a flood and a fire.**

Stopping on the side of the highway in an unsafe spot, we got out super-fast. Once it was established the bus was not going to explode, we went back in to open all the windows and doors and tried to locate the origin of the fire. There were no flames to be seen. Eventually, our noses led us to a small section near floor level where the burnt smell was coming from. We unscrewed the panel to reveal a charred 12 volt to 240-volt inverter, an essential part of the solar power system. We let all the smoke escape, waited for everything to cool down and continued homeward. *What else is going to go wrong?* We were deflated. We had paid so much for the bus and were expecting good value for money. Here we were, in less than 24 hours of ownership, with a flood and a fire.

Not a good start.

After we got home, we got a new inverter installed at significant cost. The first of many sudden expenses to come. Work started on several improvements to personalise our bus. We installed a diesel heater, LED lighting, UHF radio and antenna, new blue curtains, oscillating fans near the bed, shampoo/conditioner dispensers in the shower cubicle, rubbish bin and hanging hooks. We soundproofed the cabin and installed new carpets.

Chris engineered a whole new kitchen table that could swivel and be used outdoors as well.

A lot of thought went into picking the right name for the bus. Given its golden colour, the selection was narrowed down to anything with that colour. It was baptised 'The Golden Goose' as it seemed an omen of good luck as per the old Grimm Brothers tale. We needed a lot of luck. A specially designed decal sticker was made for the top of the front windscreen. It looked perfect.

We were so ready to go! Nothing would stop us now.

CHAPTER 3

Why is it taking so long to go?

DEPARTURE DATE OR LIFT-OFF WAS planned to be on the first of June 2022. But a series of unfortunate events made that day come and go and we were still at home.

Chris had meant to sneak in a last motorbike trip with his friend before giving up riding for a year–a difficult thing for him to do. But the original dates were twice postponed due to heavy floods all over Queensland and New South Wales. Just when the riders thought they would go, Chris' friend's younger brother passed away. This was a sad time understandably, but after the funeral, they finally set off for a 2-week dash to Alice Springs.

In the meantime, I had a disaster at home to swiftly deal with.

I had just bought our 2-year-old border collie Watson his first winter jacket as the forecast was for a cold winter. When I put it on him, he appeared fine with it. But he went running around the house and the next thing I heard was a big crash/bang sound. He had kicked the bottom part of a bay window with his left hind leg and was seriously injured. I rushed him to the veterinary hospital where he was diagnosed with two (out of three) severed Achille's tendons and needed emergency surgery. The prognosis was promising; he would regain full use of his leg. He had a screw put into his hock (ankle). However, there was a rigid protocol of recovery to be observed. Six weeks of immobilisation with on-lead toilet outings only. Then another 6 weeks of lead-only walks after the screw and the cast were removed.

The timing could not have been worse. We were delayed another week as this happened 5 weeks before departure.

I already mentioned the extensive floods everywhere. Our roof in the garage leaked and the ceiling collapsed, and in the main house the hallway ceiling was leaky. This all had to be attended to before we left, so the tenants would not have to worry about anything after we drove off into the sunset. We were so lucky to find roofers who could fix and repaint the roof and install the ceiling in the garage, with the promise to finish before we left. Could we believe them?

The stress was accumulating. Just when things could not get worse, they got worse. We hadn't found time to do a proper shakedown trip. I was still working full time. But about two weeks before departure, we managed one overnight excursion an hour away from home. That's when we woke up to a broken air suspension system!

There we were trying to get a brand-new system installed at great cost when the parts were not all in Brisbane. Our bus went in for repairs and we did not see it again for two weeks.

Meanwhile, the roofers were working feverishly away. Would they finish on time?

We were supposed to leave on a Tuesday after the final check up at the veterinary hospital on the Monday when the screw in Watson's leg was to be removed. That day, I was wondering why it was taking so long to remove the bandage. Eventually, I learned that they had found an abscess under a toe pad, which had probably contained bits of glass during the last 6 weeks and had become infected. All the attention had been on the ankle and the toes were neglected. Poor Watson. He was put on antibiotics *again* and we were to go back the next day, Tuesday, for a final checkup. Another delay of 24 hours. My nerves were extremely frayed by then. I even wondered if the Universe was telling us we should not go.

Then, finally, some good news. That day, Monday, the roofer had finished. Our tenants moved in and generously offered that we stay in the guest bedroom for the night. We appreciated their kind gesture enormously.

So off we went, finally, on Wednesday the 14th of July 2022. Big sighs of relief could be heard for a long time.

CHAPTER 4

Did you have mobile reception?

WE LEFT WITH THE SMUG understanding that we could always talk to friends and relatives. We had followed the general advice that it is better to have two mobile phones with different service providers. Chris had Telstra (Australia's largest mobile network) and I had Optus as a backup. We knew in advance that 'some' remote areas have no coverage at all, so we installed a UHF radio system 'just in case'.

Here is Telstra's coverage map from their website. We had not looked at that map before we left, believing the publicity that Telstra covers 90 percent of Australia. That actually means Telstra covers 90 percent of Australians *who live mostly in coastal areas.* Whoops.

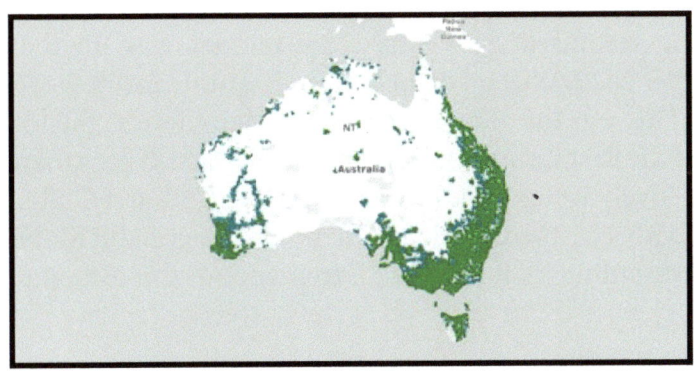

> **_Telstra covers 90 percent of Australians, who live mostly in coastal areas._**

It is easy to see now the amount of whiteness on this map where there is *no* mobile phone coverage. It took us less than three weeks to find out that there was often no way to communicate with anyone we knew. We went from a few hours to three days without any reception at all. I'd had better mobile reception in South America 14 years prior.

We learned to live with it with a few choice words thrown into the conversation here and there. We never did use the UHF. We became quite acquainted with the message on our phones 'No reception, SOS only'. Twice in the whole journey we really cursed at the phones.

The first time was on the 23rd of October 2022. We had spent the night in a free camp near Mullewa (WA). I checked my phone for messages after waking up and turning it off silence mode. There was one from my sister Diane in Montreal. It read: 'I'm sorry to let you know this way as I tried to call you but dad has passed away'. As I slept, our father had gone to sleep forever. I fell apart even though I had known the end was near. My father had been in hospital for months after a fall at the nursing home and pneumonia complications. I was in regular contact with my siblings. But that day when I tried to reach my sister Diane, the phone kept cutting out. I was devastated and so distressed that I could not speak to any of my four siblings that day. For not being there in my time of need, damn you, Telstra!

The second time I cursed the phones was on the 9th of December 2022. We had breakfast in a beautiful café near Nannup (WA). This was the second time we'd eaten there as the food was so good the first time we visited. We had poached eggs then drove on to a lovely isolated and private rest area in Karri Gully. There was nobody else there, which I will be always grateful for because, after just settling in, it hit us with tremendous force: food poisoning! We were both sick inside and outside the bus. I will save you the visuals, but believe me, it was not a pretty sight.

Chris was more affected than I and was violently ill for some hours. It got so bad; he was losing the will to live. He needed medical attention, but the phone was 'SOS only'. We had little faith that it would work, but we had nothing to lose and called the emergency number 000. After what seemed like an awfully long time, someone answered from the police department. They said they would send an ambulance to this place in the middle of nowhere.

Maybe one hour later, two lovely ambulance officers found us in the dark of the night and assisted us. They had left their Christmas party to come help us. Those two ladies will be forever in our thoughts. I stayed behind with the dog while Chris was transported to hospital. I picked him up the next day. He had been well looked after overnight in a tiny hospital. They tried unsuccessfully to put an intravenous catheter in. They gave him anti-emetic tablets and monitored him. But it took him some days to recover properly. For the SOS service you provide: Bless you Telstra!

TIPS

- Definitely have two mobile phones with different providers. Telstra for sure and another one such as Optus. It was amazing that sometimes Telstra would not work and Optus would.

CHAPTER 5

How did you handle the house chores?

ONE OF THE REASONS I was so keen to leave suburbia and hit the road was to get away from all the house chores. The endless cycle of food shopping, cooking, laundry, cleaning and emptying the rubbish had a hold on me. I was a slave to cleanliness and keeping the house picture perfect and the high-maintenance gardens tidy. Let's call it what it is: I am a neat freak. I now look back in horror at how much time I dedicated to those tasks while still working full time.

I suppose I thought things would just take care of themselves on the road and it could never be as bad as what I had been doing. Was I ever delusional. It did not take long, maybe two days, to realise that household chores travel with you, and some are much more difficult on the road. That was a slap in the face.

It dawned on me that van life was much like running a ship. I worked for 7 years on cruise ships and the similarities are uncanny. On a ship, all alone at sea, the crew are constantly monitoring the levels of fuel, drinking water, food, clean linen, power, sewerage (called black water), grey water and garbage. You definitely don't want to run out of some items, and you don't want too much of some others. Both scenarios can trigger a crisis. Therefore, there is always an element of stress when travelling along some of the most remote areas of Australia. There can be up to 600 kilometres between petrol stations and supermarkets.

Supplies and cooking

We had a pantry stocked with non-perishables in case we ran out of fresh food, which only happened once. We had a 10-litre jerry can of diesel in case we ran out of fuel (our range was about 600 kilometres), which also only happened once. There were tense moments when the solar panels were not recharging due to ongoing grey skies. Any longer and our fridge/freezer would have stopped running. Running out of fresh water is the ultimate tragedy, so we carried 20 litres extra. We were so diligent in our monitoring that we never needed to drink it. But there were many close calls with all of the above.

Unloading groceries was a job done on all fours or sitting on the floor. Even though we had a relatively big fridge of 190 litres, it was still difficult to access all the fridge areas when loading without getting down on the floor. The freezer section on top was never a problem. The kitchen cupboards needed regular re-arranging. That also was best done sitting on the floor.

Cooking on a 2-burner cooktop in a confined space was never easy. But Chris, the official chef, managed to produce incredible meals, including a cooked breakfast most days. We also had a BBQ for outdoor cooking that facilitated more delicious meals. We never went hungry. We did treat ourselves to some easy meals purchased from the supermarkets when neither of us could gather the strength to cook at the end of a busy day. We also indulged in a few restaurant outings to taste different flavours once in a while.

Washing up and stinky sinks

Washing up the dishes was done in a very small sink, being mindful not to waste water. The resulting 'grey water' is contained in a 60-litre tank. At home, the grey water just goes away in a system of pipes and pumps you never know are there. On a bus, oh you know they are there because a foul smell soon titillates your nostrils.

> *I often added bleach to the tank between emptying sessions.*

The first time we smelled that odour we wondered if we had left the toilet lid open. After a thorough inspection, it was evident the offending stench came from the kitchen sink. We had let the grey water tank fill up to capacity, so we quickly opened the valve underneath and let it drain. After that, I often added bleach to the tank between emptying sessions.

Toilets

While on the subject of foul odours, when at home, you never worry about your sewerage system unless there is a blockage. A flushing toilet is such a wonderful invention. It's so easy to take it for granted. In our bus we had a 20-litre cassette toilet. It is a removable waste-holding tank. On the road, our cassette needed to be emptied every four days maximum. And we only used it for liquids. For solid matters, we either dug a hole and buried them if we were free camping or sought out camping areas with toilet facilities. A marvellous mobile phone app called WikiCamp was the champion for that job. For $7 it was the best value purchase before we left. It tells you all the camping sites' facilities, the costs, reviews by other campers and if it is dog friendly–essential information for us travelling with Watson.

'The walk of shame' is what we called the walk with the full cassette to a dumping point. It was on wheels and could be pulled

THE PRACTICAL JOURNEY

along like a suitcase. But early on Chris broke the handle and it could not be fixed until we came back home. He had to carry it by the hand grips. That was the worst job of all. But a close second (maybe) was laundry day.

Laundry

Reality came crashing down one week into the trip with that fateful first laundry trek to the laundromat. It appears I had also taken for granted my laundry room at home. I learned the ins and outs of washing your clothes while travelling. I carried heavy bags with dirty clothes and washing detergent over long distances. I almost cried a few times when things just got too difficult: not the right coins or not enough (every machine is different and with varying costs), machines out of order, not enough space on the clothes lines to hang our clothes, too much wind and clothes spread all over the dirt on the ground on your return, no ergonomic trolley to get your clothes on the line from your basket and lots of bending down for each item, which hurt my back. I truly don't know to this day which is the worst job: emptying the cassette, which is all done in 10 minutes but twice a week, or the weekly laundry that could take hours and was backbreaking.

Housework

Let's talk now about making and stripping a bed. At home, there is nothing easier to do. You may break a nail in the process, but that should be the only difficult part. In a converted bus it is challenging. We were lucky we had a north-south island bed and could move on either side to slightly facilitate the operation. Yet it was a mammoth undertaking each week to change the bed linen. I kept hitting my head on the overhead cupboards. There was no room to manoeuvre fitted sheets underneath and over a mattress without your backside hitting the side windows. I do not know how people with east-west beds (sideways, across the van) make their bed as that needs to be done while you are on the bed.

Only one job was easier in the bus than at home: cleaning the floor. It was such a small surface that it took two minutes with a spray bottle and a cloth. There was no vacuuming, just a quick sweep with a broom. I did not mind doing that at all, and it gave some illusion of cleanliness amid the swirling red dust of the outback.

CHAPTER 6

How did you go with the dog?

WE WERE NEVER GOING TO leave Watson behind. He is a family member and very dear to us. We do not have children together, so Watson is our fur baby. Moreover, he was just a 2-year-old puppy, and you don't leave babies behind.

The unfortunate accident just before we left did complicate things and took his care to another level. He had to go through another 6 weeks of limited activity with restricted walks. We had to lift Watson in and out of the bus as he could not jump in or jump out. He weighs 28 kilograms, so this was hard on our backs. We made him a special platform so that he would not accidentally fall into the side door entrance well.

In one way, it was a blessing in disguise for him to be confined to the bus for six weeks. He would have been miserable at home stuck inside the house and not enjoying his backyard. We had already had six weeks of laying on the lounge together watching bad Netflix series after his surgery when complete rest was ordered.

Eventually, Watson recovered enough to be allowed to walk for longer periods on lead. The tendons unfortunately never reconnected properly, and the surgery failed. He now limps on his left hind leg. He does not care about it. He is not in pain. He still runs like a rocket on three legs. It was hard for us to watch him not get any better. We saw four different veterinary doctors along the way in three different states. We also exchanged emails with a professor in Perth specialising in such injuries in working breed dogs. He recommended doing the same surgery again or fusion.

> *He ran like the wind. He had the biggest smile, and so did we!*

I opted for complementary medicine as there was no way we were going to put Watson through more painful surgery and extended restrictions on his mobility. He had been through enough of that already. Watson had laser therapy, acupuncture and took Chinese herbal medicine. His gait improved slightly. Or maybe that was just wishful thinking on my part. Nevertheless, he adapted to his condition like a pro and never looked back. The first time we knew he would be okay was when he learned to navigate the tiny space next to our bed. One day he jumped up and did a sharp 90 degrees turn and came to say good morning by putting his head on the bed next to me. I will never forget that precious moment. The next time we were sure Watson was feeling better was when we finally reached Western Australia and he had his first run off leash on a deserted beach. He ran like the wind. He had the biggest smile, and so did we!

Travelling with a dog is not all fun and games though. It does limit where you can go. Most national parks are off limits. When we really did not want to miss an important national park or do a special activity, we needed a dog sitter. We learned that you could find pet sitters through online sites such as Mad Paws and Pawshake. We also found recommendations through information centres and receptionists at caravan parks. When we were running out of options, a quick message on a local Facebook community group would usually attract many responses from lovely people who just wanted to spend time with Watson. He is a people pleaser and gained so many admirers. People wanted to adopt him.

We had to be on the lookout for pet friendly areas such as wineries, tourist attractions and shops. It is amazing how many people were more than happy to invite Watson into their facilities. We have photos of him in dress shops, on a steam paddle-wheeler, on a train and in lovely vineyards admiring the scenery. Some caravan parks owners are also realising what a huge drawcard it is to be dog friendly. We estimated that about one in three grey nomads have a dog. There is a lot of money to be made catering for all the families travelling with their fur baby. We saw some parks providing hydro baths, fenced off leash areas with agility equipment, and day care. We also saw places fenced with a gate where the vehicle parks inside the fenced site to provide an even larger area for the dog to roam in. The whole family is fenced in! No doubt other caravan parks will realise that they are missing out on the pet-carrying segment unless they provide similar facilities.

Meanwhile, most caravan parks choose not to be pet friendly in the school holiday seasons. I suppose they are at full capacity months in advance, so they opt out of being pet friendly for that period. For Christmas and Easter, we circumnavigated that problem by doing house sitting. That worked out well as Watson had a backyard to run around in and we could leave him there while we did our tourist excursions around Perth and North Sydney. Everybody won.

TIPS

- Check out *https://www.madpaws.com.au/* and *https://www.pawshake.com.au/* to find a local dog sitter or put up a post on a local community Facebook page. Switch to pet-friendly housesitting in busy holiday periods if you can't find a caravan park that will accept dogs.

CHAPTER 7

What was the weather like?

WE WERE SO LUCKY TO have a lot of sunny days on our trip. We left Queensland amongst devastating rains and headed north to the tropical winter. The days were warm, but the nights were relatively cold to start with. That's what campfires are for, and we had lovely ones to keep us comfortable once the sun went down. We hardly saw any rain until, ironically, we came back to Queensland–'the Sunshine State'–almost one year later.

Western Australia was very windy for the 4 ½ months we were there. That got to be annoying after a while. We did not use our awning much as the winds were just too intense. It could easily get ripped off by a super strong gust. The winds also made cooking and eating outside almost impossible, so we spent a lot more time inside the bus to our great discontent, despite the wonderful scenery and locations.

In reality, we ended up with the longest summer of our lives, with a good nine months of decent temperatures. But when we crossed to inland New South Wales in the last month, the thermometer went south dramatically. We saw frost for the first time! It was cold, but thankfully Chris had installed a diesel heater in the bus to keep us cozy in the evening. We would not have survived without it. At night, my face felt almost frozen as I slept when the heater was turned off.

So, the meteorological conditions in general were good to us. But we saw the aftermath of major weather events in many places. It is impossible to appreciate the impact of dry and wet seasons in Australia unless you travel to see it for yourselves. We were in Western Australia in the dry season. We drove over countless unbelievably huge bridges crossing dry riverbeds. Only a few months later, the rain would flood all those gigantic valleys and those bridges would be a lifeline to keep communities from being totally isolated. Even then, the Fitzroy Crossing (WA) bridge was destroyed just four months after we drove over it by Tropical Cyclone Ellie in December 2022 and January 2023. There was also flooding of 500 metres of road, cutting access to Aboriginal communities east of the Fitzroy River as well as the East Kimberley and Northern Territory. Another bridge is being built but it will not be operational until the end of 2024.

Flood water in the same period was creating havoc everywhere. The Murray River (SA) was seriously affected before we visited, and local communities were slowly recovering from the damage. We viewed several levies that were being taken down, lots of mud still laying everywhere and debris in the trees along the riverbanks indicating how high the water had reached. So many businesses did not survive the double blow of COVID restrictions and floods. It was heartbreaking to see.

The other major side effect of the flooding of the Murray River was seen at its mouth in Goolwa, South Australia. I made quite a detour to go searching for the mouth of the mighty Murray. I was travelling alone as Chris had gone to New Zealand for two weeks. Disappointment was waiting for me there. I could not believe the stench as I got out of the bus. There were thousands of dead fish lying everywhere. It was reported that millions of dead juvenile European carp had washed up along the beaches. They are an invasive species, so in one way this natural massive culling was not a bad thing. But it was a logistical nightmare for the local councils to dispose of them all.

Cyclones are unforgiving and leave a path of destruction behind them. In Kalbarri (WA), an absolute gem of a town by the Murchison River, the devastation of Cyclone Seroja in May 2021 was visible 18 months later when we arrived. Many roofs were brand new, but many still had tarps on them. The foreshore's facilities had been wiped out and were being rebuilt. Interestingly, this is a region not normally affected by such weather systems and not classified as a cyclone risk. In the final analysis, 70 percent of the buildings were damaged or destroyed. That's an awful lot of people without accommodation.

Bushfires are a regular occurrence in the Australian summer. But the record of all times is the 2019–20 season of hellish infernos called the 'Black Summer'. Two years later as we were visiting areas that had been erased by violent fires, we could see natural rejuvenation alongside burnt-out trees that would never recover. We found Mount Hotham (VIC) looking somewhat eery with many white trees looking like ghosts on the mountain side. Yet nature always prevails, and green saplings were also visible and growing fast.

We spoke to several local people who were still homeless and living in tents on their properties or couch surfing with friends and family. It takes a lot of resilience. There are monuments in some places to thank the fire service officers and volunteers for their relentless work and service to the communities. They are the true heroes who put their lives on the line to save others.

CHAPTER 8

Where did you stay at night?

INDEPENDENT TRAVELLERS MUST FIND A safe place to stay at night to rest their weary bones. Since we were moving frequently, usually staying less than two days in the same spot, it was a constant source of tension. We only stayed more than one night in a place every 10 days or so, and usually because we were doing an excursion in the middle of the day. WikiCamp was a great resource when we had internet reception. But in the remote areas, we were on our own. We set up camp in many different weird and wonderful places, such as quarries, roadside gravel pits and farmers' fields (with permission), and next to deserted country halls. Sometimes the ones we had not planned at all turned out to be the best.

> *We always left our camp site as we found it.*

Rest areas

We stayed in many rest areas by the side of the road. You must differentiate between those meant for semi-trailers to pull into, where caravans and motorhomes are not allowed. The signage on the road usually tells you which type is ahead. Only some have toilet facilities, sheltered BBQ areas and rubbish collection while most have nothing at all. Regrettably they can be horribly messy with rubbish lying around everywhere.

The worst part is a lot of toilet paper and soiled nappies flapping in the wind. I was disgusted at the low level of decency human beings can descend to. We would drive on and not stay at the worst ones. But even in the rest areas with rubbish bins, the bins could be full and overflowing. Goodness knows how often they were emptied. Many were so remote it was a wonder that they ever were.

We met a couple who travelled from rest area to rest area in their car. All they wanted was a sheltered picnic table. They would stay there two weeks at a time as it is free. Some people are doing it really tough out there. We saw remote locations where a blind eye was turned by the local council to long-established residents who had no other options.

Wild camping

Stopping anywhere by the side of the road is my idea of wild camping. Sometimes it would be a quarry or a road base depot for the crew repairing the roads. We found some magical spots that way where we were often the only ones there. But private property is something else. You may not be aware that most of Australia is fenced off. Indeed, there was a sign in North Queensland that read 'Private property: No camping for the next 75 km'. I wondered how someone can be so wealthy to own a property with that much frontage on a major road. Graziers own a lot of land. I appreciate that free campers on their land might not be respectful of the property and damage it with campfires, cutting down trees and leaving garbage behind. We always left our camp site as we found it. We had our own little foldable brazier that was perfect and left no trace of a fire.

The best wild camping spot was on the Nullarbor crossing on top of the 60-metre high Bunda Cliffs. I will never forget the spectacular views over the Great Southern Ocean and the magnificent cliffs at sunset. There were only two other cars, and they kept a respectable distance from us as we were the first ones to set up camp. A nice young man was using a drone and took footage of us. He kindly gave us a copy of stills from the video. I still pinch myself! Look at it: We were on the edge of the world with nothing between us and Antarctica. It was surreal.

Showgrounds

We found out that almost every single little town has land dedicated to their agricultural shows. Many towns open them to campers when there are no events in progress. These can be wonderful. We have been in a few where there was nobody else around except the caretaker who came to collect the fee, normally between $5 to $35 per night. Some showgrounds are strictly cash only and no receipt. You do wonder where the money ends up. The bigger ones accept credit cards and provide a receipt.

Some people take offence if there is any horse poo on the ground. When it was the case, we did not mind. It was the least of our worries. Afterall, it was a place where horses congregate for equestrian events in the country, so it goes with the territory.

You usually get a good sleep because you are not on the side of the road and there is no traffic. But there was one place where this definitely was not the case! This was the worst place we ever stayed in: the showgrounds in Esperance, Western Australia. It was packed as it was during the school holidays, but we had nowhere else to go. Everywhere else was booked out. It was near railway tracks (which is not unusual as a lot of showgrounds are) and near a big truck depot. The noise went on all night, making it hard for a light sleeper like me. One truck driver liked to blow his horn as he went by at about 4 am. He wasn't a favourite with anyone. We were also crammed in like sardines. Chris and I both like our space around us, so it was not comfortable. Give me horse poo anytime if it means no neighbours within 20 metres.

Train yards

Australia used to depend on trains to move goods. It is incredible to see how many train lines have been abandoned since road trains took over. The advance of road constructions meant that trains were no longer economical to run and fell into disuse. Many towns have started to allow visitors to camp by the old train yards for a modest sum, usually $5 per night. There may be public toilets nearby and a water tap to fill up your tanks. At least you are guaranteed a flat spot for the night and a quiet night since the trains have stopped.

Golf clubs

We discovered that many small golf clubs raise money by letting campers stay near the clubhouse for a fee. Some provide power, access to the toilet block and rubbish collection. You are guaranteed a great view over the green golf links and a quiet spot outside the main town. They also have meals and a bar, and everyone does pretty well out of the whole arrangement. They normally only have between 6 and 10 sites. One of my favourite spots was at Mannum in South Australia. We talked to younger couples living the van life and staying on site for months at a time while working on a farm nearby. The eye-watering amount of money they were making driving air-conditioned machines made me want to get a job. The urge soon passed, but it was tempting.

Stations

In Australia, stations are what we call large expenses of land dedicated to grazing cattle, known as 'ranches' in North America. Station owners (called pastoralists or graziers) have jumped on the bandwagon and opened their doors to campers since it can be a big money spinner. We found the good, the bad and the ugly in this category. The best one by far was **Barn Hill Station** in Western Australia. It is the camping place where we stayed the longest–six nights. We kept adding one night after another as we just could not leave. It was too good!

> *The best station by far was Barn Hill Station in Western Australia.*

It had it all, perfectly positioned on top of a rocky cliff but within easy walking distance of great expanses of beach. It looked like something out of a fantasy book. The sunset views over the Indian Ocean were breathtaking. It had laundry facilities, quirky roofless outdoor showers and toilets, a small shop and entertainment at night. All that for $30 per day.

We fell hard for their delicious wood-fired pizzas (extra cost). We ordered them earlier in the day and nominated a delivery time for dinner. They were made in the main house and delivered to reception area by a driver on a quadbike. This is not your usual pizzeria set-up. Staff called out our names to announce the arrival of our warm pizza. We ate the wonderful yumminess with a glass of our chilled wine as the sun went down over another fantastic day.

But not all stations are the same. The worst one was near the southern end of the Flinders Range in South Australia. It had been recommended by fellow travellers. We showed up to this property after a hellish 10 kilometres of dirt road. That should have been a sign to stay away. We booked for two nights at $20 per night as we were still hopeful it would be okay. We were told to camp in a particular area by the creek and to watch out for their friendly cow Rosie. We asked about shower facilities and were told there was a bush shower in the middle of a dead tree. Well, the shower had not been used for a long time and was not working. It was just as dead as the tree. We were the only ones there, so we were happy about that. Rosie did come in to say hello, but she was standoffish.

It was in the dry season and super parched with not a blade of green grass. Just dirt and plenty of it. But the worst part was the grass seeds everywhere, getting into Watson's fur, our shoes and our clothes. Spear grass seeds are just the worst thing for dogs as they dig their way into their skin, paws, ears and eyes and can create terrible infections and wounds. They have a painful sharp tip that can easily penetrate through the skin. Even worse, they have a barb that fans out and makes it impossible for the grass seed to go backwards–like the tip of a fishhook. Once they get in, they just keep moving in deeper. It took us hours to remove them all.

We all hid inside and Chris and I declared that we would leave the next day at first light. We could not get out of there fast enough.

In between the worst and the best stations were some nice ones along the way. They try to attract tourists with different tactics. One had hot Artesian spa baths in big tubs. Many offered bush walks that led to points of interest such as a river or a cliff. Some offer sunset spots with a table or a bench so you can take a drink there and enjoy the view for happy hour.

Caravan parks

We were not keen on caravan parks when we started our journey, and we still aren't. To us, they were the antithesis of freedom–a type of suburbia on wheels we wanted to avoid at all costs. We could not think of anything worse than dozens of caravans closely stacked side by side in street-like fashion. But they grew on us as a necessary evil when there was nowhere else to go or it was laundry day.

There are many standards amongst the caravan parks. Some chains are meticulous and provide top-of-the range accommodation. We were first introduced to the **G'Day group holiday parks** in Katherine (NT). The first impression was a good one. And it lived up to it. We were pleasantly surprised by the space between campers and the cleanliness of the ablution blocks (for showers and toilets). The park was also covered in green grass–something we had not seen in over one month. This was in the Northern Territory where red dirt reigns. It had a small pool, which we plunged into as soon as we could as the weather was hot.

Along the way, we stopped at a few more G'Day parks, but we initially refused to become a member as a matter of principle. We were determined not to be locked in by marketing gimmicks, even though it is cheaper for members each night. It was not until we were in South Australia, 5 months later, that we finally relented and joined. We got our membership fees back in the next two weeks with the 10 percent discount each time. How silly were we to have missed out for so long? After that, we quoted our membership number everywhere. Principle, what principle?

I still have nightmares about some of the lower-level caravan parks we stayed at. The independent owners who do not belong to a franchise can have such different approaches. Some will go the extra mile and provide a most beautiful environment with a pleasant welcome at reception. One even had fresh flowers and bathmats in the bathroom. *Bathmats!* A luxury not seen anywhere else. On the other hand, many had clearly passed their due date. They looked like they did when they first opened in the 1960s, with no renovations having been done at all. The ablution block could be out of a horror movie with spider webs in the corners, cracked tiles and red dirt stains in the showers. As they say, you pay your money and take your chances.

TIPS

- I am not getting any commission for highly recommending: *https://www.barnhill.com.au/*
- And for goodness' sake, become a member the first night you book in: *https://www.gdaygroup.com.au/*

CHAPTER 9

What does off-road mean anyway?

WE WOULD HAVE LOVED TO buy a large 4WD motorhome, but it was outside our budget. Still, we were under the impression that Toyota Coasters could go anywhere albeit slowly because they have a higher ground clearance than the average factory-built motorhome. They also have four driving rear wheels and a large, legendarily robust diesel engine. I had read many posts on a Facebook Coaster group on that subject. Photos of Coasters in all kinds of terrain inspired me that they could go anywhere. Chris had not seen them, and he was not as enthusiastic to hit the road, forgive the pun.

> *Everyone has different definitions of 'good dirt road'*

The first day on the road was almost our last day. We had been advised that the road to the caravan park we were heading for had a 'good' dirt road of only 5 kilometres. This is when we realised that everyone has different definitions of 'good dirt road'. For us this was a highway to hell. It had potholes like moon craters, and it was 35 kilometres long. Did we take a wrong turn? That was the last time we took road advice literally. To be fair, it possibly was not that bad in a 4WD. But we were novice Coaster drivers with hope in our hearts and a new air suspension that we wished to keep for the entire trip.

In retrospect, we were initially going too fast, at 50 kilometres per hour, over the deep corrugations and potholes. Everything was shaking, including poor Watson who was petrified. We seriously thought the bus was going to disintegrate or explode. Either way an unpleasant prospect. We slowed down to 5 kilometres per hour and the journey became almost bearable. There were a few choice words exchanged between husband and wife in the tense moments. We did make it to the other end of the road in one piece. If only I could say that was the hardest part of the trip…

We were to encounter many more bad roads and much longer ones. Some are ingrained in our memory for all the wrong reasons. We could not circumvent them as they were the only way to get from A to B to avoid backtracking. One example is the 'sealed' road between Normanton and Burketown in northern Queensland. This is part of Highway 1, the national motorway around our magnificent country. We had great expectations of decent driving conditions. That section is 225 kilometres of potholes and dilapidated bitumen. We thought it would never end. It took us over 5 hours to navigate. We had seen much better dirt roads. We still cannot believe that a national highway can be in such a state of disrepair. It was our point of reference from then on and nothing was ever as painful as that road.

The road between Gregory and Camooweal (QLD) was a testing one. That was 222 kilometres of unsealed road, so we were prepared mentally for a rough ride, unlike Highway 1 above. But we stopped counting, after 47, the number of blown tyres we saw by the side of the road. It gives you an idea of how bad it is. Still, we managed to get through that segment without too much hassle, just very slowly in some sections. And our six tyres survived the ordeal.

The real 'off-road' experience worth mentioning was taking the 'Goose' cross-country to the top of the Mary Kathleen abandoned pit site where radioactive uranium was once mined. The open-cut mine opened in 1956. By 1963 the major supply contract had been satisfied and the works were closed down. However, it was reopened in 1974 with Mary Kathleen's second life extended to 1982 when reserves were finally exhausted. The land has since been rehabilitated and is now suitable for grazing. We did see plenty of cows in the paddocks. Unfortunately, it is now known that the tailings repository at the Mary Kathleen site has been subject to seepage of radioactive waters at rates much higher than initially predicted. Poor cows, but I digress.

The only way to the stunning blue (radioactive?) lake is up a tortuous road. We debated whether we would be crazy to attempt it. But we are not easily deterred and up we went over rocks, brushing past trees and manoeuvring near deep gullies on the narrow track. I will never forget the faces and dropped jaws of drivers in their 4WDs equipped with every accessory known to humanity coming down the other way. Their big eyes indicated complete disbelief and wondering if they were hallucinating. *Is this really a bus coming this way?* It was not so funny at the time–it was truly stressful–but we can laugh about it now. We made the trip to the pit fine, but on returning Chris made an error driving into the campground over the washed-out bridge. It cost us one tyre, which was replaced in Cloncurry by the helpful tyre agent. The crazy drive had been definitely worth it to take the potentially prize-winning photo.

The only place we did not feel confident was in deep sand. We knew we had to be careful camping close to the beach on sandy ground. Sometimes we could feel the front wheel bog down and the rear wheels start to spin. At those moments, timing, momentum and power were our friends. Chris drove those bits, where his motorcycling and outback driving experience came to the fore. That was scary enough, and we never attempted to go straight onto a beach even though I had seen photos of Coasters parked on the sandy beaches. The recovery of a 5-tonne bus from a lonely beach could present significant problems. We knew how far to push our luck, and Mary Kathleen had been right on the limit.

CHAPTER 10

What are we doing tonight?

THE DAYS WERE LOADED WITH sightseeing and filling all our senses with memorable inputs. We also had daily problem-solving of different issues to keep us on our toes. Watson needed his exercise and to be attended to with lots of cuddles. But once we had dinner, the dishes had been done and everything put away, what did we do for entertainment at night? It really depended on where we were stationed.

> *Opportunities await travellers who keep their eyes and ears open.*

In a secluded spot on a clear night and with just a bit of a chill in the air, sitting by a campfire and stargazing was top notch entertainment. If we had mobile reception, I would use an app on my phone to identify stars in faraway constellations. We would talk about everything and anything and solve all the world's problems, with or without an alcoholic drink. We never went to bed late as we were usually so tired from the long full days.

In a caravan park where campfires are not allowed, that was a different story. If we had television reception, we might watch the news and maybe an interesting program. But we are not TV watchers and commercial channels annoy us with their constant advertising. In any case, we rarely had television reception. We often remembered a man we met at a roadhouse when we crossed into Western Australia. We commented to him on how beautiful the mountain ranges were, and he remarked 'Oh, you like that? Well, there's plenty more coming your way. Same old same old, brown and green and blue all the way. All I want is a bakery and good TV reception. You should stop at the next place. There's good TV reception there'. We quoted him repeatedly and laughed our heads off as we continued our travel without much TV reception, which we obviously couldn't care less about.

We had a video player and had brought three DVDs with us. One of the joys of travelling was finding that often there are books and DVD exchange spots in service stations, libraries, second-hand shops, cafes and caravan park reception areas. We took advantage of those whenever we found one. Our three DVDs and two books kept getting recycled. Discovering one of those trading posts and seeing what was on offer was exciting. The titles might not have been our usual selections, but we expanded our horizons and discovered some gems and some laughable duds.

Some caravan parks provide entertainment at night. It may be a big bonfire with someone playing the guitar. It may be a couple of comedians who pass the hat around at the end of a very funny evening.

We attended the most wonderful concert by the world-acclaimed classical guitarists Grigoryan Brothers who happened to be touring regional cities. They had composed and released an album of 18 original works–*This is Us: A Musical Reflection of Australia*–inspired by objects they had found at the National Museum of Australia in Canberra. We could not believe our luck when we saw that they were going to play the night we were in Dungog, New South Wales. Moreover, it was held in the James Theatre–the oldest purpose-built cinema still operating in Australia. It is a magnificent building in the Spanish mission style with a gleaming white-and-red façade. Our cup runneth over.

Slava and Leonard's musical responses to the iconic artifacts they picked took us on a stirring journey through Australia's history and heritage. It was a moving concert and we felt so privileged to listen to it. There were only 80 people in the audience. Can you believe it? These two brothers usually fill concert halls. Wonders never cease and such opportunities await travellers who keep their eyes and ears open.

We were also fortunate to attend a bush poetry recital by the award-winning Gregory North at the North Gregory Hotel. No, that is not a stage name but his real name. He was the male Australian bush poetry performance champion in 2008, 2009 and 2010. From May to September each year, he is the resident poet at the local hotel in Winton (QLD). Chis had seen him before and was keen to see him again. His show is a mixture of history and poetry. We learned so much about Waltzing Matilda and Banjo Paterson. It was another night to remember.

On special occasions, we would go out to dinner to a nice restaurant. They could not be too upmarket as we did not have anything fancy to wear. We found some wonderful establishments with great food. We are both food lovers and like to try new taste sensations.

We additionally provided our own entertainment by enjoying happy hours, playing Scrabble and Word Jumble on our iPad. I also had my daily contribution to the travel log on my Facebook group page, which included reviewing and editing my photos. There was always something to do and we never got bored. We were a self-contained unit, and even in campgrounds we were not regular attendees at the large gatherings of caravanners.

CHAPTER 11

Did anything scary happen?

OVERALL, AUSTRALIA IS A SAFE place to travel through, even though the media makes you believe we inhabit the most dangerous country on Earth. Indeed, here live highly venomous and scary animals. But not once did we see a scorpion, a snake or a shark, even though I am sure sharks were in the waters where we swam. We saw crocodiles on a cruise down Nimitluk (Katherine) Gorge, but even that did not make us feel threatened at all. On the other hand, there were incidents that raised our blood pressure and when brown corduroys would have been appropriate pants to wear.

One night in Gladstone Jetty (WA) was a scary one. We'd had our fair share of blustery days in Western Australia. It is no wonder the state is covered with wind farms. At last count, there are 15 wind farms delivering over 1,000 megawatts of power. This night in Gladstone was memorable. The winds got up to over 60 kilometres per hour. The whole bus was rocking wildly and shaking. Loud clapping noises made us jump. We hardly slept. We thought the solar panels on the roof were about to be ripped off. At times it felt like the bus itself was going to lift off, with us in it. It was very scary. We held on to each other and wondered if we would make it to the morning. We did.

THE PRACTICAL JOURNEY

Bushfires and road trains

The Old Boab Tree campsite in Western Australia was the site of two scary events that stand out in my mind. Firstly, shortly after we arrived there, the air was hot and there was smoke in the distance. As time went on, the smoke clouds got darker and closer. We listened to the news on the radio (thankfully we had reception) and learned there was a big bushfire in Derby where we were headed.

Bushfires are a part of every Australian summer. They can start suddenly, move quickly and affect large areas. Typically, Western Australia's bushfire season runs from June to late October in the Northern Region. This was 28 August 2022. Bushfires can be devastating and have a lasting impact on communities. People have been killed or seriously injured and homes destroyed during bushfires.

There were about 10 other campers on site, and we were all discussing what to do. Should we turn around or stay put? The wind was pushing the fire away from us, but we knew that could change in an instant. We all decided to stay put, watch and be alert. Small ashes were falling on us, so we were quite concerned. We managed to get to bed but everything was in place for a quick exit if required.

As it turned out, the scariest thing that night was not a fire but a huge road train. We were woken up by a semi-trailer passing between the Boab tree and us, at a distance of maybe 30 centimetres. The ground shook and the noise was deafening. It did not slow down and just kept going. We can only assume the driver wanted to stop for the night but noticed the place was full of campers and continued on. Thank goodness the driver was skilled and managed not to hit us. If we had left our chairs and table out as usual, he surely would have hit them in the dark and driven them into the side of the bus. It's a miracle he did not hit the bus. We counted our blessings that night.

An annoying incident involved an LPG road train with three trailers. We were sleeping in a rest area by the side of the road near Pardoo in Western Australia when we were awoken by the said vehicle parking right next to us. The driver had decided this was his overnight stop too. The pumps and machinery on the trailers kept going and made a terrible racket, to which he was seemingly oblivious. We did not know what to make of it and certainly could not sleep. Unlike the previous incident, this truckie didn't care about people camped there trying to sleep. So, we took off in a hurry and drove in the dark (which we usually never did) for about 15 minutes until we found a deserted spot by the side of the road. He could have done the same. We are sure that the people we left behind wouldn't have slept a wink, but for us it was sleep take two.

The scariest part of Australia is the wide-open road. We came across a lot of road trains. In Western Australia they can carry up to four trailers and dwarfed our 7.2 metre-long bus. Of course, they went much faster than we did, and many passed us. The drivers we saw were all highly skilled professionals. It was always a nervous moment, but nothing beats being confronted with an oversized truck carrying mining or farming equipment coming in the opposite direction. They are accompanied by pilot cars–one at each end–and a police escort with lights flashing. They can take up the *whole* two lanes of the road. They normally are loaded with gigantic mine equipment travelling from one site to another.

> *The scariest part of Australia is the wide-open road.*

On the Eyre Peninsula east of Kimba (SA) we came across one of those monsters. The police car coming in the opposite direction in our lane made it obvious that we *had* to pull over on the side of the road NOW. Unfortunately, that was easier said than done as it was a narrow shoulder. We were almost pushed off the road, but we managed just in time to stop somewhere safe.

West of Camooweal (QLD), a red ute passed us at an amazing speed. I nearly had a heart attack! I had been constantly checking my side mirrors and did not see that one coming at all. It came out of nowhere. It went by like a missile, with its shock wave hitting the side of the bus. Chris estimated the speed was over 200 kilometres per hour. It was well over our horizon in seconds. The whole experience left me shaking for quite a while.

Locusts and runaway dogs

Another road hazard that was totally unexpected was a swarm of locusts crossing the Nullarbor. There are no words to describe the sound of hundreds of big grasshoppers, up to 8 centimetres long, crashing loudly against our windshield. We were under attack! One minute they are all on the bitumen and the next minute they are coming at you full force. One wonders why they would go on such a suicide mission. There are things you can't unsee, and the splash of those many dead bugs in front of us made for poor visibility. Turning on the wipers only made things worse until finally the washers sprayed water over the debris. The hellish vision lasted a few minutes, but it was repeated a few times along the way. The first time was the scariest without a doubt. Cleaning up the mess afterward was a challenge and a sickening task.

Other events scared us but for totally different reasons. Our dog Watson was the source of great fright on two occasions. Hearson Cove is an idyllic beach in Western Australia. For us, Hearson Cove went from heaven to hell in a matter of hours.

At high tide, it's an ideal swimming spot, and at low tide, you can walk for hundreds of metres on the exposed tidal flats. We visited at low tide, and thinking that we could swim, we walked out a few hundred metres and found that we were still only in knee-deep water. The beach is dog friendly, and Watson was frolicking in the water nearby. Suddenly he decided to just run like crazy to the other end of the beach, maybe one kilometre away. Unfortunately, that was when Chris found out he had lost his wedding ring! I had to leave him trying to find his ring while I dashed after Watson. He decided to turn it into a chase game and headed further out to sea. No matter how much I screamed at him to come back he just went further out. I was so worried at that stage as the tide was coming in fast. Because the land was so flat for so long, he was at great risk of drowning as he could never swim back fast enough to beat the incoming tide. I could not go in either as I would be in the same predicament.

I tried to walk away in the other direction, hoping he would come back in, but he ignored me, possibly thinking this was great fun. He had been locked up in the van for two months, always on lead when outside as he was recovering from his ankle surgery. This was his chance to be free. Chris eventually noticed we were both gone and came to the rescue. With his deep voice, he commanded Watson to come back, and Watson finally did as he was told. Phew! That was a close call. Poor Chris never found his ring.

Watson gave me another big fright on a beach at Minnie Water in New South Wales. He spotted a young Staffordshire bull terrier and decided to have a big run with his new friend. Off they went into the distant far reaches of the beach, not a care in the world. Then a 4WD drove by and caught up with them. This was not a 4WD beach and it should not have been there. But there it was, and Watson and his doggy mate had no road sense at all. He does not know that cars can hurt him. So, there they were zooming in and out of the vehicle's path and all I could do was watch in horror. I thought that was it. He was going to get run over. But the 4WD turned around and the new game was over. Watson stayed behind with his friend, and I walked calmly towards him to get him on the leash. It was no use being mad at him as he had no idea how close to death he came. This dog is so frustrating when he is disobedient and won't come when called!

Not-so-scary ghosts

The most ironic thing was that something that was advertised as terrifying ended up being underwhelming. We are talking about the most haunted pub in Australia, the North Kapunda hotel. We did the nighttime visit, the Kapunda Ghost Crime tour. The history of the pub is interesting. The hotel was opened in November 1849 as the North Kapunda Arms. It had many name changes until it went back to its original name in 2010. As an aside, the pub was the site of the first reading of the Riot Act in South Australia from the hotel's balcony. Anyway, ghost hunters think the pub is home to several malevolent spirits.

It is reported that a woman was murdered in one of the rooms by a man known as 'the man in black' (no, not Johny Cash!). He is believed to be one of four spirits that haunt the premises. We never saw a ghost but some rooms did feel a bit weird. One fellow tourgoer was really into it and sensing spirits all around us. Perhaps she just drank too much spirit, who knows? Maybe that was just a demonstration of the powers of persuasion. Either way I would not recommend the tour.

CHAPTER 12

Why do we keep getting injured?

AT THE BEST OF TIMES, I am clumsy and often hurt myself accidentally. I bump into things as my personal spatial awareness is deficient. Chris is not as bad and does not bruise easily. However, we both hurt ourselves so often during our journey that I thought it might be worth discussing how it happened so you can avoid the same things.

> *At times I thought the 'harmless'
> Goose was out to kill us.*

The bus is full of hazards that we were completely unaware of until we travelled in it. At times I thought the 'harmless' Goose was out to kill us. Some injuries happened to both of us and others were our own individual assaults.

For a start, we both repeatedly hit the top of our heads on the cupboards in the kitchen and above our bed. You would think after one hit, we would be more careful. But no, it kept happening because we were in a rush to get something out of a cupboard and not paying attention. It was worse for Chris who is taller and thin on top, and he would cut his scalp open. They were just minor injuries, but they still hurt. Two other areas were notorious for head butts: the top of the staircase area and the ceiling behind the seats where there is a small bump. At least they are padded areas and less painful.

Our poor heads suffered more pain when the door was up in the boot/trunk area. We would forget it was open and as we came around the corner of the bus, BANG! We would hit it full on the forehead. OUCH!

Then our heads, necks and shoulders would get hurt whenever getting up from ground level near the awning arms attached to the bus. Usually that was when feeding Watson and filling up his water bowl. Once again, we would forget the awning was open and make contact unexpectedly, accompanied with a few expletives.

We both also got hit in the head or face when opening the driver's door in the morning, forgetting there is a shade leaning in the window at night for privacy reasons. It would fall on us. It is not heavy, but it always took us by surprise and irritated us more than anything else.

Then there were the steps. Our first set of steps were the original ones that came with the bus. They were wobbly and we would often misplace a foot and fall off them. The step up was not very high, but it is a miracle we did not break or twist an ankle. After four months of tolerating the shaky steps, we finally bought a better 2-step in a camping shop in Western Australia. I am amazed by how patient we were with those first dreadful steps.

Most accidents happened when stationary. But once, when we were driving, I had to get up to find something in the kitchen cupboard. I know I should not leave my passenger seat when travelling, but the road was smooth bitumen and it looked safe enough to do so. I was standing in the hallway getting ready to open the kitchen cupboard overhead when the bus lurched sideways over a bump in the road. I headbutted the cupboard door with a big cracking sound. I know I am a hardheaded woman but that was a most unpleasant incident. I quickly went back to my seat feeling sad and sorry for myself.

While on the subject of overhead kitchen cupboards, I got hit in the face many times by falling objects after opening a door. Everything moved in the cupboards when we travelled on rough roads. Even though I had lined all surfaces with non-slip mats, items were stacked up and would dislodge in transit. The first time was with a glass bottle of vitamin supplements. I got more than my dose that day. I relocated the offending bottle to somewhere else where it could never hurt us again.

What else happened?

I broke countless nails opening stiff windows and ceiling vents. The window tracks were full of dust and became hard to open with the friction. I cleaned them up and sprayed silicone to make them smoother to operate. Thank goodness I had read somewhere to always carry a can of silicone spray in the outback. But it would only last a few days and the tracks would be gritty and uncooperative again.

Chris had an unusual encounter. He caught his finger in the fridge door handle as he walked by. Being a large guy, he has great momentum and nearly tore his finger off. It was a one-off incident, perhaps due to a lapse of balance.

Of course, there were burn injuries from cooking with gas. Chris almost set himself on fire once by spraying cooking oil on the BBQ grills after turning on the gas.

There was the splintery task of finding wood to burn in the campfire. But that was nothing compared to the near fatal attack (I might be exaggerating here) of hundreds of spiders that exploded out of a log Chris was cutting up with an axe. They did not bite us, but they certainly frightened us as much as we frightened them. Our heart rates went up for sure.

But we did get bitten by insects of all kinds. I am highly allergic to insect bites, and they always swell up and are very itchy. I still have scars on my lower right leg from unidentified culprits. I never saw what bit me on two separate occasions. We suspected a type of spider. The sites became inflamed and hot and itchy for weeks.

The midges in the north of Western Australia were unusual. They had white dots on them and a good bite from one gave us a month of an itchy recurring lump. We also got bitten by March flies and mosquitoes. One night we hardly slept as we kept getting up to kill mosquitoes that had invaded the bus. They seemed to multiply as we attempted to sleep. We wondered where they were coming from.

In Preston Lake (WA), which strangely enough is a beach, a freakish wave came out of nowhere and I was smashed down in the sand. Many other swimmers also got badly dumped by this relatively small shore break. One solidly built gentleman nearly broke his neck. We all got out at the same time and compared injuries. I was sore all over for a few days.

Considering all that happened, we came home without any serious injuries bar minor cuts, bumps and bruised egos. We were lucky indeed.

TIPS

- Always pack a can of silicone spray when travelling in the outback.
- Don't walk through the van when it is on the move.
- Mind your head and have a big first aid kit easily accessible.

CHAPTER 13

How did that break?

BREAKDOWNS ARE PART OF ANY lengthy road trip. We knew that mechanically the Goose was perfect and would get us around Australia without any issues. The trusted engine 1HDFTE is arguably the best ever produced by Toyota. We had heard so many horror stories of other engine breakdowns and blown gaskets. Our engine delivered without a hiccup. But it was other things that broke down and gave us grief.

The expensive pneumatic suspension system we installed just before leaving stopped working three days after departure. We called the company that had installed it and they understandably said they could not help us unless we returned to Brisbane. That was not going to happen. So, Chris spent hours under the dashboard with a multimeter looking at all the electrical connections. Thank goodness he has electrical engineering qualifications. After checking everything, he found that the system had been wired to the radio! We had turned the radio off as reception was non-existent where we were. Once we turned the radio back on, we heard the familiar pssssssssss sound of air bags adjusting to the level. So, we continued on our journey. Unfortunately, the system never worked perfectly. We had air leaks and would wake up with the side door lower and unable to get out, with the steps in the way. And the worst part was the drain on the car batteries. We did not know then that this was why our batteries kept packing it in.

We had installed two new 12-volt batteries soon after buying the bus. Yet a few months into the trip, one battery went flat. We got a new one under warranty. We thought that maybe there was something wrong with it. We had a flat battery many months later due to leaving the lights on. So that was easy to fix with the local garage recharging the batteries. A few more months went by, and we were enjoying a nice stay by a lovely lake in Western Australia. We were getting ready to go and the batteries were flat again though no apparent reason.

We extended our stay for another night and called for help. The local auto electrician diagnosed a flat battery (out of two). It was replaced at great cost. By then we are wondering what is going on. Finally, in Dubbo (NSW), near the end of the trip, batteries were flat again. This time we were informed that batteries should always be changed in twos. We were lucky that one battery was replaced under warranty, but we had to buy the second one. I was furious at that stage. The auto electrician there expressed his concern with the air suspension system wiring as it was apparently continuously draining one battery. We'd been set up for failure from the start. There were phone calls to the company owner in Brisbane who said they would reimburse the costs and make the necessary mods to the system upon our return to Brisbane (which they did at their cost). We soldiered on.

The Goose has six tyres, including four on the rear axle. It is not officially a 4WD but has four driving wheels. We did not expect to cover that much ground without changing tyres due to wear and tear. Nevertheless, we did have a few unexpected incidents where new tyres had to be purchased such as that climb up to Mary Kathleen Mine (Chapter 9).

The fridge gave us a lot of stress. It would defrost one day and start again the next. We would throw all the food out of the freezer that we could not eat quickly and replenish. It happened a few times until it finally stopped working. We were in Mount Isa (QLD), a place we did not really want to stay longer than needed. Unfortunately, the only auto refrigeration place with good reviews had three days wait before we could be seen. So, we parked ourselves on a caravan park's footpath, which was their overflow area when they were fully booked. We managed to occupy ourselves somehow with touristy things.

Finally, the day arrived to get the fridge checked out. It had started working again, but we wanted to find a solution once and for all. We can't blame the technicians as they tried their best to diagnose what was wrong with the fridge and its intermittent fault. As far as they were concerned, the thermostat was fine. They sold us two other parts in case the fridge stopped working again and showed Chris how to put them in. They did not have a thermostat in stock. We were headed for remote areas and *needed* refrigeration. After spending $550 there we were none the wiser, and the fridge stopped again later on. By then Chris had already ordered a thermostat at a place we were driving through in a few days' time, just in case–the only one left in Western Australia. He changed it himself and the fridge never had any other issues. My hero to the rescue once again!

Water is essential. When it appeared we had run out, despite closely monitoring all the time, we hit the panic button. It turned out that the water pump had stopped working. While in Perth we bought a new one and Chris replaced the old one. But of course, it rarely goes as planned and the new one was faulty, so it was replaced under warranty. Why is it so hard to get things to work when brand new? I despair at the low quality of products these days, but they are cheap. I guess we just had the bad luck to pick a

THE PRACTICAL JOURNEY

dud one off the shelf. Fortunately, the new one did not miss a beat for the rest of the trip.

Another issue was the door lock on the driver side not working properly. Sometimes Chris would be locked in and would have to exit through the side door. It was kind of funny. He tried to fix it to the best of his ability on the road, but we were moving almost every day with little time to attend to it. I thought it was sticking with all the dust and sprayed it with my trusted can of silicone. It would behave for a while, but the same problem would reappear with the lock jammed in. It is only when we came back home that Chris had a closer look at the mechanism in the door by removing all the panels. He found that a crucial spring had broken. He replaced it and it is now like new, clicking open and shut as it should.

Overall, all these things were simple and relatively minor when we put them in perspective. We know of people who were held up for weeks in remote areas at the mercy of the local garage, waiting for parts to arrive from the big cities. We cannot complain. It was all part of the rich tapestry of travelling in a 20-year-old bus.

CHAPTER 14

How much did it cost?

IT IS ESSENTIAL TO HAVE a general idea of how much a lap of Australia will cost before you set off. We had read about people cutting their trip short after running out of money. We did not want that to happen to us.

> We were not going to miss out on some once-in-a-lifetime opportunities.

The budget must allow *for a lot* of unplanned extra costs, which are bound to happen. Australia is a notoriously expensive country to travel around, and we were not immune because we were Australian. We had read that most people would spend $1,000 per week. There are a lot of factors to consider: the number of people travelling together, the type of rig used (petrol versus diesel), accommodation, the type of food eaten, happy hour drinks (which can be expensive in the outback), tours and entertainment. Your level of comfort is paramount and will dictate your final costs.

Budgets can vary between super cheap such as that of Tony Mangan who walked and camped around Australia (see Chapter 18) or super extravagant. The latter is called 'credit card travelling' and that says it all. One travels in a car and stays in hotels/resorts and eats out all the time. Our budget was between those two extremes, to suit our needs.

Fuel

We had chosen a large diesel-thirsty vehicle. Fuel consumption varied from 15 to 19 litres per 100 kilometres depending on the terrain and the wind. The average price was around $2.50 per litre, which was still expensive compared to unleaded petrol prices at the time. We paid up to $3 per litre on the Nullarbor crossing. We used a petrol app to determine prices at the various Nullarbor fuel stops. By planning where to stop based on price we saved over $100 on the crossing. Though sometimes we had no choice. Beggers can't be choosers as there can be a long distance until the next petrol station. You pay whatever the amount is because you really don't want to run out of fuel.

The total cost for fuel was almost $12,000 for 33,280 kilometres. That is an average of 36¢ per kilometre.

Accommodation

The second most expensive item was accommodation. We stayed in 70 free camps, which included friends' places. We also did two house sitting sessions. The first one was over Christmas, south of Perth for 10 days. The second one was in North Sydney for Easter over 14 days. We also splurged on a few Airbnb's just to give ourselves a break away from the bus on special occasions. For my birthday we stayed three nights in a beach shack in Horrocks (WA) for $300. The next extravagance was 5 nights in Silversands (WA) in a beach house for $1372. It was worth it.

Chris had to fly to New Zealand and stop to see family in Brisbane on the way back. He was gone for two weeks. But we agreed to stay together for one week before he left in a holiday house in Yankalilla, South Australia, to explore the Fleurieu Peninsula. The total cost for 20 nights there was $2,600. It was the best way for me to stay in a safe place that was also pet friendly. Chris did not want me to stay in a caravan park on my own.

The rest of the accommodation varied in price from $5 to $140 per night. (Chapter 8 has more details about our overnight stays.) *The total cost was almost $11,000.*

Adventures and sightseeing

Chris and I are both adrenaline junkies. I have done bungee jumping, parachuting, hang-gliding, scuba diving, whitewater rafting, jet boating and water skiing. Chris has been a motorcyclist for 50 years and has made some risky moves. On our trip, we indulged in some serious fun activities, but they were expensive. We did not skimp on things we really wanted to do while we could still do them. We knew that there were areas we probably would never go back to. We were not going to miss out on some once-in-a-lifetime opportunities. Here is a detailed list of our most unusual daredevil activities in descending order of cost.

1. HORIZONTAL FALLS, DERBY (WA) CRUISE

The most exorbitant item was the Horizontal Falls tour from Derby, Western Australia. It involved a thrilling low-level seaplane flight over gorgeous Talbot Bay then a magical boat tour to the amazing Horizontal Falls, the only place in the world where such a phenomenon occurs. We had to be there at the right tide to get the best spectacle. We visited the Horizontal Falls in the afternoon. It was exhilarating and worth every cent. We were then welcomed onboard a floating houseboat pontoon for an indulgent evening, enjoying sunset drinks (BYO) on the deck, fresh Barramundi for dinner and breakfast the next morning. This was followed by another trip to Horizontal Falls. They delivered exactly what they promised: 'Excitement, wonder and peace in one overnight stay'.

The price for all the above was $2,134 for two people including scenic flights there and back.

2. Lake Argyle and Bungle Bungles National Park (WA) scenic flight

Due to a big mix up, a cruise on Lake Argyle (WA) we had booked was cancelled. We were a bit stunned but quickly recovered when we found out we could do a flight over Lake Argyle and all the way to the Bungle Bungles National Park, which was not even on our radar. The 2-hour scenic flight took us on an unforgettable adventure, showing us so much more than the lake cruise would have done.

We flew over the Bungle Bungles Range, Lake Argyle, the Argyle Diamond Mine and the whole Ord River Irrigation Area. We also saw the stunning Carr Boyd Ranges, Osmand Range, the Ord River and the Bow River. Lake Argyle is Western Australia's largest and Australia's second largest freshwater man-made reservoir by volume. It is definitely better to see it all from the air to appreciate how big that lake is.

The cost was $890 for the two of us: such a bargain!

3. Swimming with a whale shark at Ningaloo Reef (WA)

You cannot explore the Ningaloo Reef, Western Australia, without swimming with the biggest fish in the ocean: a whale shark (which is neither a shark nor a whale). Nothing can prepare you for the amazing experience of being near these gentle giants. Every year, between March and July, up to 600 whale sharks congregate in the reef, making it one of the best places in the world to spot whale sharks. They can grow up to 18 metres in length, with a mouth over a metre wide that is designed perfectly for consuming plankton and krill. They are completely harmless to humans. If they swallowed you, it would be by mistake and hopefully they would spit you out.

There was only one juvenile whale shark swimming around. He was about six metres long but was still impressive when he was right in front of us. So close we felt like we could touch him. They have such beautiful patterns on the skin. Naturally, we followed up by buying our new mascot–a stuffed whale shark toy we called 'Ning', which sat on the dashboard for the rest of the trip.

We visited in the off season and the price was lower, at $660 for the two of us.

4. Wild Adventure to Dirk Hartog Island in Shark Bay

One of the most beautiful wonderlands in Australia is Shark Bay (WA). There we joined the 'Wild Adventure to Dirk Hartog Island' tour. We enjoyed morning tea sitting at the Inscription Cafe with spectacular ocean views. We then jumped on a heart-stopping 4WD excursion to the west side of the island to view the outstanding landscape, Blow Holes and Surf Point marine sanctuary. Have you ever heard of nervous sharks? That is where they live by the thousands. They are called nervous sharks because when they brush by each other, they quickly dash away from each other, starting a chain reaction like an atomic explosion. This is so funny to watch in the clear blue water. If they could talk, you would hear 'sorry, oops, sorry'.

It was a great day out and worth $550 per couple.

5. Waco biplane flight in Fleurieu Peninsula (SA)

We loved the Fleurieu Peninsula of South Australia for so many reasons. But the highlight without any doubt was the Waco biplane flight. Built in 1992, the Waco is a modern-day version of a classic 1935 sports biplane. It has a huge radial engine and is unique in its ability to carry two passengers in its capacious front cockpit. It was a privilege to fly in one of those gorgeous flying machines for 20 minutes. We zoomed over the Fleurieu's beaches and vineyards like millionaires. We even wore leather helmets.

(Biggles, eat your heart out.) We just couldn't wipe the smiles off our faces. It was great value, and I would do it again in a flash!

We paid $490 for the two of us.

Nitmiluk (Katherine) Gorge

A Nitmiluk Gorge tour is a must if you are travelling in the area. We did the Nimitluk 2-gorge tour. It was mesmerising, with a wow moment every few minutes. It is very wild country with deep orange cliffs towering overhead. The cruise boat takes you to a landing station and you go for a short walk to admire the cliffs up close. It is definitely not for people with mobility issues.

The cost was $415 for two.
The rest of our tours ranged from $10 to $100 per person.
The total cost of all tours was nearly $10,000–a hefty sum to be sure.

Food and incidentals

We love our food, and we ate well. But overall, we spent about the same amount as we would eating at home. There were other incidentals such as:

- LPG refills for our two bottles (used for cooking and hot water supply)
- pet sitter fees when required (mostly for the activities listed above)
- bus maintenance such as

  - 2 sets of front tyres
  - 3 changes of oil (every 10,000 kilometres)
  - a new fridge thermostat
  - new car batteries.

When I added it all up, it was a surprise to find that we spent roughly around $1,000 per week. This was the average I had read about, and it proved to be true in our case. We could have made it a lot cheaper by doing more free camps, but when you get close to civilisation caravan parks are the only choice. Our options were limited due to travelling with Watson.

Total cost

We need to add the devaluation of the Golden Goose when we sold it as well as the cost of insurance and registration. The total loss was over $20,000, which equates to an extra $400 per week. Most people will lose a lot less when they sell their rig at the end.

I still think we did well, and the reality is that such an adventure is priceless. It costs what it costs to make it happen. We believe we got great value for our money, and we travelled in super comfort.

While on the subject of cost, one factor to consider is the concept of 'payoff' for all the efforts you put in. This is totally different to the cash you spend. In the first month, we often found that we were just driving endlessly, spending a fortune on fuel and not getting much back in terms of payoff. Let us be honest: some parts of Australia are not exciting. The scenery is boring and interesting activities limited. When the distance between destinations is very long, you may have to decide what to prioritise. Driving on will get you there faster, but you will be disenchanted. Your mood will turn sombre, and you will wonder what you are doing. If on the other hand, you decide to stop somewhere that is uninspiring, by the side of the road, at least you will get to rest. It is not all about the money, honey!

The question at the end is *'Do you feel that the payoff is worth all the time, effort and money you put into the trip around Australia?'* Our answer is a resounding yes. The payoff is not a dollar sign but a deep feeling of satisfaction and pride.

PART 2
The Magical Journey

It is all very nice to be practical and organised, but the real trip started after we left home. I had dreamed about what it would be like. I would lay on the bed in the bus and visualise our trip ahead whilst waiting for one more delay to get resolved. But once we left Brisbane, the adventure began in earnest. I often felt like we were on a magic carpet ride during our Big Lap of Australia. We were 'flying by the seat of our pants' on that carpet most of the time. This led to some extraordinary findings in unexpected places. It truly was magical in many ways. This part of the book will show you why.

CHAPTER 15

Where are we going?

'WHERE ARE WE GOING?' IS a question we asked ourselves almost daily. We did not want to just drive around National Highway 1. We had already explored a lot of our home state Queensland's coast. The goal was to spend most of our time in the farthest states, Western Australia and South Australia. The original itinerary was quite vague. We had only planned the first three days out of Brisbane and the general direction we were heading: northwest.

We left home around 11 am and figured we could drive about four to five hours before needing to stop for the night. **Biggenden** was our first destination, where we opted for a caravan park with reported mountain views. We had not made a booking, so we were left with the last site with views to the ablution block. It was a disappointing start and the first of many undesirable views from our motorhome. But let's not dwell on that as we had a lot more breathtaking views in the final tally.

The second night was in **Monto**. I just had to visit that town since it is where my best friend Carol spent many years in her childhood and adolescence. I had heard so much about the place from my conversations with Carol over 25 years of friendship. It is a lovely town and campers can stay in the abandoned railway yards at the bottom of the main street for a mere $5 per night. Surprisingly, fires were allowed and the firewood similarly cheap.

The third stop on my 'must see' list was **Biloela**. This town made national news when the local population rebelled after the federal government of the time decided to send a Tamil family to a detention centre. The family had been deemed 'illegal immigrants' after living and working in Biloela for three years. The town rallied around them and worked tirelessly to bring them back home. It took four years and a change of government to make it happen. I had followed their story closely. I admired this rural community who had embraced this family in the great Aussie tradition of giving people a 'fair go'. I knew they deserved our tourist dollars. We had breakfast in a lovely restaurant and there was a friendly vibe in the air. It really is worth stopping there and supporting such a caring community.

After Biloela, it was pure coddiwompling. The first time I saw that word was on the back of a caravan in front of us when we had yet to leave Brisbane. I had to look it up in the dictionary.

'Coddiwompling' means travelling purposefully towards a vague destination. Supposedly, it comes from the southern states of the USA. It is now one of my favourite English words along with 'flabbergasted' and 'serendipity'. Coddiwompling was precisely what we were doing; every day was a surprise. We would peruse the atlas (my travelling bible) or Google maps when we had mobile reception. Later we would collect tourist brochures from information centres and refer to them for inspiration. I have kept all those brochures: 3 boxes full. We would look up names and attractions to see where we would go next. Some places were wild goose chases and got us nowhere. We also exchanged must-see spots with fellow travellers going in the opposite direction. That revealed some gems. Sometimes we would just follow a sign on the road to a point of interest.

I loved the uncertainty. I felt like a modern-day explorer. When I was young, I used to jump on my bicycle and just go explore my neighbourhood. I suppose I have not lost that sense of discovering what is around me. It is a never-ending search. There

WHERE ARE WE GOING?

is always something new to look at. Our final itinerary is shown in yellow on the map below.

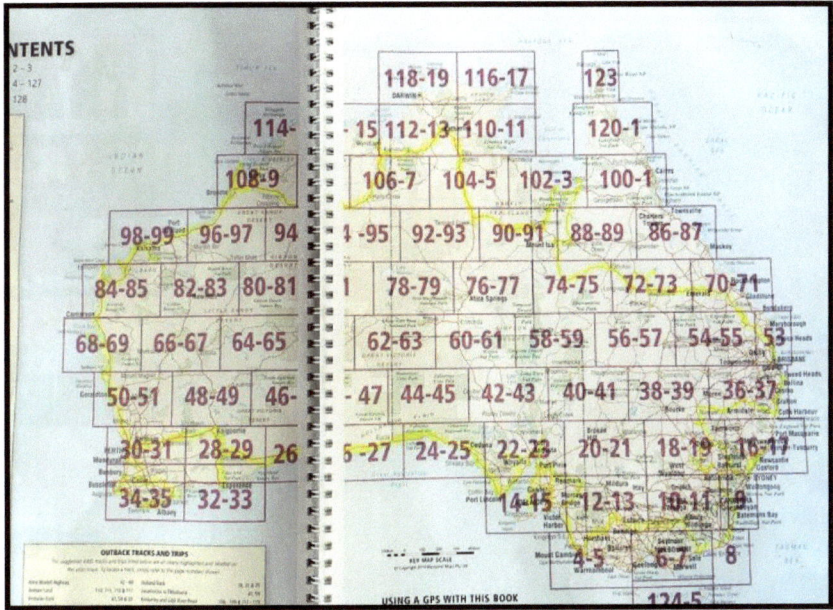

I have decided to categorise the places we visited in the following chapters instead of listing them in chronological order. My mind works like that. My pantry, my bathroom vanity, the rooms in my house, all have categories. I also organised the bus with different categories to make it easier to find things at the beginning. I had the dog section, the paper product section, the alcoholic drinks section, the hot beverages section, the pharmacy section and so on.

CHAPTER 16

Did you see that?

AUSTRALIA IS A BIG COUNTRY full of 'big things'. Have you ever heard the expression 'Go big or go home'? That could be Australia's motto. The propensity to build 'big things' started in the 1960s. Today there are more than 600 big things across the country. We certainly saw plenty of what some may label 'tacky' tourist attractions along the way. I prefer to call them quirky works of art or novelty architecture. But some do stand out in our memory.

The Tree of Knowledge

In Barcaldine, Queensland, situated on the junction of the Capricorn and Landsborough Highways, a most unusual 'tree' awaits you. It used to be a real tree–a ghost gum (Eucalyptus Papuana) with a significant history.

The tree, which grew outside the Railway Station, became the meeting centre for the Great Shearers Strike in May 1891 when protestors gathered under its branches. About 3,000 shearers marched under the Eureka flag to protest against poor working conditions and low wages. Now called 'The Tree of Knowledge', it is a heritage-listed icon of the Labor Party and Trade Unions

Unfortunately, in 2006, the old tree was fatally poisoned by an unknown villain. Miraculously, the tree's remains were taken to Brisbane for the world's first preservation process. It was then returned to Barcaldine and placed under an artistic timber construction. The box-structure is made from 4,913 individual timber pieces, of which 3,449 are hung to give the illusion of a canopy over the tree. From the outside it just looks like a huge square box suspended in the air. But when you walk underneath and look up to see the canopy, it is a whole different story. Serenity enveloped me as I stood under that tree. I love forests and trees and the fact that this is not a real tree did not matter. You can feel that the spirit of that tree lives on as a great symbol of Australia's political and social history.

The Big Easel

An amazing sight in Emerald in the Central Highlands is the mega artwork of Van Gogh's sunflower painting. Artist Cameron Cross built the 25-metre-high easel upon which the painting sits using about 13.6 tonnes of steel as part of his project to have 7 sunflower sculptures in 7 different countries. The painting was unveiled in 1999 and remains the world's biggest rendition of a Van Gogh sunflower painting. Sunflowers are my favourite flowers. The artwork represents Emerald's pride in being a major producer of sunflowers. It reminded me that I once had a reproduction of the painting in my apartment in Quebec City in 1984. I had borrowed it from the art collection, which at the time was a new concept. You could borrow more than books from a library. I thought I was so sophisticated back then!

The Big Barramundi

Everywhere in North Queensland, fishermen long to catch the elusive large freshwater fish called a barramundi–the most common species found in the Norman River. The Big Barramundi in Normanton is one of Queensland's most famous big things. Constructed in 1995, it is 6 metres long, and one of three sculptures dedicated to the barramundi found around Australia. That is one popular fish. I don't fish but I do like the taste of barramundi.

The Big Crocodile

It's extraordinary that Normanton can claim a second big thing! This one was definitely more exciting than the Big Barramundi. There is an 8-metre-long fibreglass saltwater crocodile named Krys the Savannah King. It is a replica of the largest recorded saltwater crocodile ever captured in the world. Sadly, the unlucky crocodile was shot nearby in July 1957 by Krystina Pawlowski. The crocodile oddly was named after her (who thought of that?). Krystina and her husband were famous crocodile hunters in the Gulf region. She ended up regretting the kill after realising that they couldn't use the skin as he was too big to move and too old to use. She had a complete change of heart on the matter of crocodile hunting after this and dedicated the rest of her life to conservation. At least something good came out of that meaningless killing.

The Big Stubby and the Pink Panther

We did not spend much time in the Northern Territory (NT) unfortunately. But it was enough time to see a most unusual tourist attraction. The Big Stubby sculpture sits outside the Larrimah Hotel beside a pink panther in a chair. The Northern Territory Draught stubby comes in a massive 2,270 millilitres (over two litres) bottle nicknamed the Darwin Stubby. Why such a big bottle? Northern Territory Brewery started in 1956 and without a bottling plant in Darwin, it shipped bottles from Melbourne. With nearly 4,000 kilometres to transport the beer, the brewery decided to introduce the Big Stubby in 1958. The Northern Territory Draught Darwin Stubby finished regular production in 2015.

I am not a beer drinker and was horrified at the size of that bottle when I first saw it. To see an even bigger version was unexpected. To see it matched with a giant pink panther defied all logic. But that's the Northern Territory and the Australian bush sense of humour.

The Big Camera

Meckering in Western Australia is a must-stop town for a few reasons. We had heard of the devastating earthquake of 1968 that had flattened the town. It was 6.5 on the Richter Scale–the second strongest quake recorded in Australia. Thankfully, it happened on a public holiday and not many people were in town. So only 20 people were injured. On the other hand, many buildings were damaged. Before the quake, Meckering had 51 dwellings, 12 businesses and 15 public buildings. Only 16 houses and 3 businesses survived. You can still see the fault line that created so much damage. It was originally 32 kilometres long and, in some spots, two metres tall. The earthquake ripped the earth open. One kilometre of the fault line has been preserved in the farming fields. The rest has been ploughed flat. We found what was left a bit underwhelming considering the catastrophic damage that it caused. It was hard to see, so don't waste your time looking for it like we did.

You might like the Big Camera though. Built to resemble a 35-millimetre SLR camera, it is hard to miss. It hosts an amazing collection of earthquake photographs and old newspapers clippings. There was no charge to look at those. But there was a cost to see the only museum in Australia totally dedicated to photography. I am a keen photographer, but for some reason that day I had had enough of museums, and we didn't go in.

The Big Wool Wagon

The Big Wool Wagon was a surprising find when we arrived in the town of Kojonup, 56 kilometres south-east of Perth. That is when we learned that the wool industry had a significant impact on the area's development. In the 1840s, early European settlers brought flocks of sheep to graze on the fertile lands around Kojonup. By 1969, there were over one million sheep in this shire.

The sculpture was constructed in 2001. It is a one-and-a-half-size scale model of an old wool wagon used to transport large quantities of wool from markets and depots in Perth. Horses were harnessed to the front of the wagons and the loading required great strength and labour from the local farmers. Look at how it dwarfs Chris in the photo.

Stonehenge

I never knew there was a Stonehenge in Australia. Chris, who was born in the United Kingdom, lived as a child close to the original Stonehenge ruins. He used to play amongst the stones when younger. I have always wanted to visit the original Stonehenge. It was with great delight that we made our way to this tourist attraction near Esperance (WA). It did not disappoint. It is the only full-size replica in the world. It appears as the original would have looked around 1950BC. It consists of 137 stones of local pink granite that were all quarried from across the street. They say the natural stone provides an energetic feel and the circular shape amplifies sound. It is an amazing place to visit.

The layout consists of a circle containing a horseshoe within a horseshoe. Each stone weighs between 8 and 50 tonnes. The highest ones are eight metres high and there is an altar stone. Just like the original, they all line up with the summer and winter solstices in Esperance. Walking around the site on a cloudy day makes for an eerie experience.

The Big Kangaroo

Crossing the Nullarbor can be a bit monotonous. It was with great amusement that we spotted something new when we went over the South Australian border from Western Australia on the Eyre Highway. Welcoming us was the 'Big Kangaroo Rooey II' at Border Village. It is a five-metre-high sculpture made out of papier mâché and fibreglass.

Only in Australia will you see a big kangaroo promoting a big jar of vegemite (it used to be a can of beer) and allowing people to jump in the pouch. Classical Australian humour at its best. I respectfully abstained from jumping in.

The Big Lobster

The Big Lobster is a tourist attraction in the town of Kingston SE, in South Australia. Known as 'Larry the Lobster', the impressive orange sculpture stands 17 metres tall. It was built locally in 1979. Larry was recently ranked No. 1 Best Big Thing in an Australian Broadcasting Corporation (ABC) rural poll. It is actually quite scary to look at and not pretty at all.

The Loaded Dog

The Loaded Dog was such a quirky discovery as we drove past Whyalla Veterinary Hospital (SA). We did a U-turn just to have a closer look. His name is Tommy, and he is the size of a small horse. Scottish sculptor Andy Scott created him in 2007. It is made up of hundreds of small steel rods welded together.

I just loved the big goofy dog with a toy in his mouth. Or what I thought was a fetching toy. I did not know it was based on a fabulous story by Henry Lawson titled 'The Loaded Dog'. It is a tale about three gold miners who use explosives to blow up shafts. One day, their dog Tommy, a retriever, steals a stick of dynamite and runs around the camp creating havoc. After that incident Tommy is always chained up. The story is so funny to read. Do not be alarmed. No animal is hurt in the story even though there is an explosion.

The Big Windmill

I love windmills (but I do not chase them!). When we arrived in Penong in the far west of South Australia, I thought I had died and gone to heaven. There is an open-air museum of windmills, which includes the biggest windmill in Australia. It was built in 1932 and used until 2003 when the fan of the windmill was destroyed by high winds. The Penong locals resurrected and restored it in 2016. The windmill is commonly called 'Big Bruce' after the owner Bruce Nutt who has loaned the windmill to the museum. It is one of only fifteen 35-foot Comet windmills ever made and one of only two erected outside of Queensland. 'Big Bruce' is unique compared to the other Comets as it has a span larger than the standard 35-foot fans (closer to 37 feet). The windmill is capable of drawing water from 150 metres deep and pumping over one million litres of water a day. And all in an environmentally friendly way.

There are over 20 windmills in the collection with many brought back from ruin. There is a photo display showing before and after shots.

We sat on the special swing among the windmills that at first seemed out of place. Looking closer, we saw that the swing is rigged with a similar mechanism to windmills. It pumps water as you swing. How clever!

The Big Galah

A giant eight-metre-high bush bird is perched out the front of a service station in Kimba, which is reportedly halfway between the west and the east coasts of Australia. The Big Galah is dwarfed by the soaring 30-metre-high grain silos nearby. Its bright pink colour and design are eye-catching.

The Big Wine Bottle

It was a complete accident that we spotted the first big thing in South Australia as we had missed a turn to go see something else. The town of Rutherglen is a magnet for wine lovers and that is why we were there. We never expected to see a giant wine bottle, but there it was like a beacon on the landscape. This giant roadside attraction is a nice recycling of a 72,000-gallon disused water tank sitting atop a tower. It was originally the community's second water supply. The Wine Bottle became a big thing in 1969 when a mesh top section was added to turn its original cylindrical shape into a wine bottle.

Map the Miner

We already mentioned Kapunda for its infamous Ghost Tour. But it is also where you can find Map Kernow, the 'son of Cornwall'. Map the Miner represents the Cornish copper miners who once worked in the area. Standing seven metres tall at the southern entrance to the town, the work was built by Ben van Zetten and opened on 5 June 1988. The statue was destroyed by a fire in 2006. It was completely rebuilt by the same artist within 12 months with funds from the insurance company. How unusual is that?

The Big Golden Guitar

We are not country and western music fans, but we could not resist the appeal of the Golden Guitar in Tamworth (NSW). At 12 metres tall and weighing half a tonne, it is an Australian icon. It was officially opened in 1988. The guitar is made of fibreglass over a steel frame. It is a replica of the smaller trophy presented to artists at the Country Music Awards held each year. That is why it has no strings.

The Big Banana

Opened in 1964, the Big Banana was one of the first big things in Australia. It is located in a highly visible position on the Pacific Highway in Coffs Harbour. Originally, it marked a banana plantation. Now the 13-metre-long landmark is accompanied by a fun park with laser tag, a giant slide, mini golf, ice skating, a toboggan ride and a water park among other attractions. We just drove in front it and that was enough for us. A little too touristy for our taste.

The Big Merino

Built in 1985, the Big Merino is a monument to Goulburn region's wool industry. Anatomically correct, 'Rambo' weighs 100 tonnes and is 15.2 metres high and 18 metres long. Once a pit stop for those travelling through Goulburn, the Big Merino's popularity suffered when the Hume Highway was re-routed to bypass the town in 1992.

But in 2007, Rambo was relocated 800 metres closer to the highway so he could once again enjoy the spotlight. His three-storey interior contains a permanent exhibition on the 200-year history of wool in Australia as well as a gift shop and an observation area where visitors can experience Rambo's eye view. We only saw it from afar and did not venture inside.

The Big Prawn

Ballina's 33-tonne Big Prawn was constructed, without a tail, atop a service station in 1989 as a nod to the local prawning industry. The sculpture fell into disrepair and was facing demolition when the service station closed in 2010. Thankfully, Bunnings Warehouse came to the rescue. When the hardware group moved in, $400,000 was spent restoring the prawn, even adding a 16-metre tail. The Big Prawn now cuts a remarkable figure next to its saviour. There is another Big Prawn in Exmouth, Western Australia. Just like Larry the Lobster, I find that a bit intimidating to look at.

CHAPTER 17

How many stars are there?

I HAVE ALWAYS LOVED LOOKING at the sky and stargazing. I will get up in the middle of the night to spot unusual astronomical events such as comets and meteoroid showers. I note in my diary lunar and solar eclipse events. Travelling in outback Australia provided endless opportunities for beautiful starry nights. When we were all alone and there was no light pollution, truly the sky was the limit.

At last count, there were 201 certified Dark Sky Places in the world. These are places that have an exceptional quality of starry nights and nocturnal activity and may be protected ecologically. For example, Australia has three accredited Dark Sky Places in conservation areas: Warrumbungle National Park (NSW), the River Murray Reserve (SA) and the Jump-Up Sanctuary (QLD). They each provide stargazers with a superb view of the stars, the Milky Way and many other beauties out in space.

Isn't it a surprise that Australia does not have more dark skies? It's true that much of Australia has pristine stargazing conditions. But rural areas are under threat as a result of mining and oil or gas production.

There are three types of sky viewing areas: sanctuaries, reserves and parks. Sanctuaries are in remote locations. Reserves have a core area with sky quality and natural darkness, and a peripheral area that supports dark sky preservation in the core. Parks are more accessible to the public and still feature exceptional starry nights.

Warrumbungle National Park, near Coonabarabran (NSW), became Australia's first Dark Sky Park in 2016 and the first in the Southern Hemisphere. Stargazers and astronomers have been flocking there since the 1950s. The area has crystal-clear night skies, low humidity and high altitude, all of which contribute to excellent sky viewing. There is a world-class astronomy research facility at nearby Siding Spring Observatory with Australia's largest telescope. This impressive telescope is open to the public. It has a café and great views. Definitely worth a look.

A museum called the **Jump-Up** near Winton in Central West Queensland became Australia's first Dark Sky Sanctuary in 2018. They have an average of 58 cloudy days per year and only 31 days of rain, which makes perfect conditions to see the stars in all their shining glory. The museum also has the largest collection of Australian dinosaur fossils in the world. It gets booked out quickly and we did miss out as we did not want to hang around Winton for days on end. So be smart and book ahead.

Australia's newest Dark Sky Place, on the Murray River, was designated in 2019. **The River Murray Dark Sky Reserve** is remarkable since it is just 100 kilometres from Adelaide. Its dark skies are supposedly some of the darkest anywhere.

We missed out on visiting the sites in Queensland and South Australia. So it was with great delight that we approached the best spot for stargazing in the Dark Skies Park of New South Wales. **Coonabarabran** and **Narrabri** offered us magnificent viewing at night. We did the stargazing tour and looked at nebulae, constellations, the moon and black holes through powerful telescopes. It was mind blowing. And the answer to 'How many stars are there?' The latest research estimates there are 20×10^{23} stars in the corner of the universe that we can see with our current telescopes. That is two septillions for people who prefer names for large numbers.

Isn't the cosmos a wonderful place? It's the ultimate big thing and to see it, all we have to do is look up at night.

CHAPTER 18

Did you meet anyone interesting?

WHAT MAKES A PERSON INTERESTING? I feel that, just like beauty, it is 'in the eye of the beholder'. But nobody can deny that Australia is known for being full of interesting characters, some home-grown and some born overseas who migrated to Australia for a better life. Many are extraordinary and some even notorious. I present to you my list of interesting people we met on our trip.

Tony Mangan

The most exceptional person we met was just passing through. We first saw Tony Mangan walking purposefully, pushing his faithful companion Karma–a 3-wheel cart flying an Irish flag–along Highway 1 in a westerly direction against the traffic. We passed him on the other side of the road as we were also heading west. He did not look in need or distressed in any way, so we did not disturb him. But I did feel bad that we did not offer him water at least. We stopped a few hours later for our overnight stay. It was

THE MAGICAL JOURNEY

by the magnificent big old Boab tree, mentioned in Chapter 11, on the way to Wyndham (WA).

In the morning, I noticed the lone walker sitting under the shelter having breakfast. I thought this was my chance to go and see if he needed anything. I found that a nice couple in a caravan next to him had already supplied him with coffee and refilled his thermos with hot water. He did not want anything else from me, saying he likes to keep Karma light so that it is easier to push on uneven roads. He said he would appreciate it if I could take his rubbish with me as there were no garbage bins around. I gladly did so. I went back to the bus to get my husband.

We introduced ourselves, and he gave us his business card, which indicated that there was much more to the small fit man in front of me. First, he cycled around the world. That was not enough. Between 2010 and 2014, Dubliner Tony ran around the world, totalling an incredible 50,000 kilometres. He was raising awareness for mental health. This involved running roughly the distance of a marathon per day. Now he is simply 'walking' around the world to raise awareness for early cancer detection. He is currently the holder of the world 48-hour indoor track record at 426 kilometres. He is also the world 48-hour treadmill record holder at 405 kilometres.

That man is a force of nature. He is now 66 years old and shows no sign of retiring. Chris asked him how his blood pressure was with all that exercise. He smiled and responded in his soft Irish accent that it was 'pretty good'. He is humble and such a nice guy to talk to. Of course, I now follow his travels on Facebook and you can too. Just ask to become his friend https://www.facebook.com/tony.mangan.14.

Karstan and Maxine

We met fellow travellers doing incredible journeys of their own. We encountered one couple with a 2-year-old daughter at Barn Hill Station in Western Australia. They had what looked like the most beaten-up 1968 VW Kombi van you have ever seen. In fact, the vehicle was tip-top, but they had retained an old patina on it. They turned out to be Australian celebrities, but we did not know of them. Karstan and Maxine became famous when they participated in the reality TV show *The Block* in 2014. They are documenting their travels through social media. They have taken that van everywhere.

Karstan was sociable and pleasant to talk to. Maxine was busy keeping up with social media entries and minding their daughter (the latest news is that they have had another baby daughter). We can only envy their lifestyle, doing what they want to do at such a young age. We felt old and wondered why we had worked so hard for so long and waited till retirement to live the dream. But to be honest, for them it's still a job and they work hard videoing, editing, flying drones and so on. They are not the only family doing it. Plenty of people are on the road with kids and dogs in tow, doing home schooling and picking up work as they go. The spirit of adventure is alive and well in this country.

You can follow Karstan and Maxine on: *https://www.facebook.com/KarstanAndMaxine/*

Julie and Kim

They say it is hard to make new friends as you get older. But we did just that when we met Kim and Julie onboard the Pemberton Tramway in Western Australia (now permanently closed). We glanced at each other on the tram but met again afterwards at the nearby Big Brook Dam. We chatted and learned they were on a long weekend escape from Perth. The next day we found out we were staying right next to their cabin at Fonty's Pool Caravan Park. We ended up having the best happy hour together and talked for hours. We told them that we would be near Perth in a few weeks' time, and so we planned to meet again.

We reunited for Chris' birthday on the 22nd of December. It was just the four of us and Chris had the best 70th celebrations considering that we were far away from family and friends. Julie and Kim were so hospitable and generous. They were just strangers a few weeks before and now we are friends.

They invited us to see the New Year in with them at their place. That is when we discovered through general chit chat that Chris had known Julie's brother for 25 years through motorcycle riding. Her brother James had even been a guest at one of our parties! The world is indeed small when things like that happen. Kim and Julie are precious gems, and we certainly consider them interesting people! They have an unusual backstory but that is for them to tell.

Harvey Dickson

We saw the signs to Harvey Dickson's Country Music Centre and were curious. Located five kilometres out of Boyup Brook (WA), it was once open to the public. But now entry is only by appointment with Harvey. He was free to show us around and so our private tour began.

Harvey's place is a melting pot of country music, rodeo, entertainment, memorabilia, Elvis and farm life. There is original art everywhere including an assortment of animals sculpted out of wood. Three 15-metre Guitar Men stand tall and proud, which started out as trees growing in the wild. There is no other place like it. Harvey could not have been more welcoming as he walked us around his property. In the country music indoor stage–a *huge* shed–there is stuff on the walls and hanging from the ceiling. It is overflowing and overwhelming.

It all started when Harvey's grandfather founded the farm in 1886. Harvey as a teenager always had a dream to host a country music event on the farm. It took him 20 years to make it happen. Since 1969, every February he has hosted the annual event. His wife Rose was an integral part of the organisation. Sadly, she passed away in October 2017.

Harvey asked us if we had time to spare. We said we were retired and had plenty of time. He then spoke fondly of his wife and how things were not the same without her. You could tell he was lonely and enjoying having someone to talk to. Harvey took us to his inner sanctum and played us some of his favourite Elvis records. He put on a 'special record' he was sure we had never heard of. He was right. It sounded like Elvis, but it was American singer James Hodges Ellis. His voice was so similar to Elvis Presley's that Ellis and his record company played upon it, making some believe that some of his recordings were by Presley, or even that Presley had not died in 1977. He started using the stage name 'Orion' in 1978.

Ellis always dyed his hair black and wore a small mask and similar clothing to that worn by Presley. Orion had several hits on the country music charts. Then the story takes a weird turn when Ellis tore off his mask at a performance in 1983, saying he would not wear it again. However, after failing to retain his popularity using his real name, he returned to performing as Orion in 1987.

Sadly, in 1998, Ellis was murdered during a robbery in his pawn shop in Alabama. I would have known none of that if we had not met Harvey Dickson. With his permission I took a photo of him sitting in the amazing Presley room. He's a great guy.

Gary Muir

Gary Muir totally mesmerised us when we went on his two-and-a-half-hour eco-cruise on an overcast day, departing from Walpole in Western Australia. We had been told that it was good entertainment, but it went beyond our wildest expectations. The man is a hyperactive genius and the skipper of the vessel run by his company Wow Wilderness. This is a family business that started in 1910, when nobody else was even thinking about conservation.

One of Gary's memorable quotes is 'There is the North Pole, the South Pole and then Walpole, the belly button of the Earth!' We will never forget Walpole now. Our brains actually hurt after listening to him talk non-stop. He had data on everything and recalled everything without notes.

Gary is also a historian and a published author. In 2010, he started to co-write *Tolstoy to Tinglewood: The Case of Frank Skinner Thompson* with his friend Geoff Fernie. The book is a fascinating account of papers found in an old boatshed in Walpole. Gary travelled to Russia for research, riding the Trans-Siberian railway and crossing the Gobi Desert on a folding bike. On this trip, he narrowly avoided arrest by police officers curious about the infamous papers he was carrying.

But back to the cruise and Gary's jam-packed information session. It was more than a lecture; he was also performing theatrics. He has so much knowledge in his brain that he just wants to share with everyone, in a fun way. He is extremely passionate about nature and conservation, dedicating his life to it. He wants everybody to make better informed decisions about the biosphere and their role within it. He is additionally a comedian. Did you know that the fairy wren has the biggest testicles in the whole animal kingdom? When it is time to mate, they can swell to 25 percent of their body weight! See the photo of Gary giving us a visual insight. Talk about entertainment. He is a hard act to follow.

Pleun Hitzert

There are several people we wish we would have met in person, but at least we could visit the results of their genius and hard work. Some people might call their projects follies, but I call them truly inspired masterpieces.

At the top of the list is a windmill we came across by accident as we drove past. It was not mentioned in any of our tourist brochures. It is the **Lily Dutch Windmill in the Stirling Range (WA)**. The five-story full-size Dutch windmill, with its 22-tonne cap and 24.6-metre sail length, is one of the largest traditional windmills ever built in Australia. A brick round-sail flourmill, it is functional and still produces flour for local farmers.

The man behind this project is Pleun Hitzert. His health is unfortunately failing, so he recently appointed a new manager to take over. The windmill is not open for tours, but we were lucky that the manager saw our interest (remember, I love windmills) and offered to show us through. We were delighted and impressed no end by the mammoth effort required to build such a mill. Pleun has many strings to his bow, being a professional saxophone player–we bought his CD and have listened to it many times–an entrepreneur, a pilot, and a restauranteur. From 1991 to 1997, Pleun singlehandedly assembled the windmill brick by brick on his property, from second-hand bricks at that. You hear of such people and then reflect on what you have done with your own life. Pleun certainly does not waste a minute of his time on this planet. He leaves a great legacy, and I am sorry we did not get to meet him in person.

Chester Osborn

Another genius in my book is the creator of the **d'Arenberg Cube in the McLaren Valley**, South Australia: Chester Osborn. The idea to build the d'Arenberg Cube came to Chester in 2003. He combined the puzzles of winemaking and Rubik cubes. Each of the five levels have been carefully designed to entice the senses, including a wine sensory room, a virtual fermenter, a 360-degree video room and many other tactile experiences.

We spent four hours in the Cube, and we could have spent another four easily. Chester is a fourth-generation winemaker and such a creative man. It appears there is no end to what he can visualise. He has his fingerprints on every aspect of design in the Cube. Even the toilets are a work of art and planned by him. We, of course, did not get to meet the man as he is too busy running his empire. We were simply in awe. It would spoil the experience if I told you more. It has to be seen in person.

Vittorio Stefanato

A migrant who dreamed big is Vittorio Stefanato. We visited his **Amigo's Castle in Lightning Ridge (NSW)**. We were so impressed by this man's hard work, dedication and passion. This most unusual building–described by some as bizarre–is truly a work of love.

Vittorio arrived in Australia at the age of 22 in 1970. In 1973, he called Lightning Ridge home. Needing somewhere to live, he thought stones would be a cheap and sturdy building material for a small camp. He was not a qualified builder and was self-taught. Well, some 40 years later that modest camp became the Castle and an international tourist attraction. Unfortunately, the council declared the site unsafe and stopped the progress on the mansion. As you walk around the place you can see why some parts are unsafe and not accessible to tourists.

We learned from the tour guide (a family friend) that a tragedy happened here in 2020 and a woman was shot. The circumstances around the event are controversial and have divided the local community. Vittorio pleaded guilty to murder and was sentenced to 18 years in jail in February 2023, a few months before we visited. What an end to his Australian dream.

Prince Graeme

There is one interesting person we really wanted to meet. It was Prince Graeme of the **Principality of Hutt** in Western Australia. We looked everywhere for this property that had made the news for over 50 years. The story is unbelievable.

The principality was a regional tourist attraction. It issued its own currency, stamps, and passports–all non-valid. It all started when Leonard Casley declared his farm to be an independent country (sovereign state) on the 21st of April 1970. With an area of 75 square kilometres, it was larger than several countries. He attempted to secede from Australia over a dispute concerning wheat production quotas. A few years later, Casley began styling himself as 'Prince Leonard' and granting family members royal titles.

The principality was never recognised as a country by the Australian Government. Legal battles were fought for decades in the High Court of Australia and Supreme Court of Western Australia who both rejected submissions arguing that the principality was not subject to Australian laws.

In February 2017, at the age of 91 and after ruling for 45 years, Casley abdicated the 'throne' in favour of his youngest son Prince Graeme. On 3 August 2020, the principality was formally dissolved. The Australian Government was chasing 50 years of unpaid taxes. The property was sold to recoup the money owed. Everything was demolished and the land has returned to wheatfields. That is why we could not find it anywhere. It does not exist anymore. What a saga!

CHAPTER 19

How weird was that?

WE CAME UPON REALLY BIZARRE stuff as we moved along from state to state. I wrote them down in my notebook as I did not want to forget them. And because I thought nobody would believe us when we talked about it. It almost seems like fantasy, but it is nothing but the truth. The whole truth.

Alcohol police

We found out that alcohol laws vary between states and even between towns in the same state. The Northern Territory took us by surprise in that department. The tourism brochures rave on about genuine outback Australia. Tennant Creek in the Barkly Tablelands, known for its million-acre cattle stations, gold mining heritage, iconic rock formations and Aboriginal culture, sounded like a great place to visit. Australia's last gold rush took place in Tennant Creek in the 1930s, earning the town its title of 'The Territory's heart of gold'. We enjoyed the underground tour at the Battery Hill Mining Centre, which houses Australia's last operating 10-head gold stamp battery.

But driving through town itself was not inspiring. We arrived just before 4 pm and saw people circling the liquor store. We discovered that the local opening hours to purchase alcohol were strictly between 4 pm and 7 pm. Buying takeaway alcohol is never easy in the Northern Territory. Every customer must produce a valid form of photo identification to prove they can legally make an alcohol purchase. Since February 2023, changes to Northern Territory liquor laws have included even more restrictions about:

- times and days takeaway alcohol can be purchased (not on Sunday)
- how much of certain types of alcohol can be purchased daily such as no more than *one* of the following:

    - 30 cans x mid-strength or light beer
    - 24 cans x full-strength beer
    - 12 cans or bottles x ready-to-drink mixers
    - 1 x 2 litre cask of wine
    - 1 x bottle of fortified wine
    - 1 x bottle of green ginger wine (13.9 percent alcohol)
    - 2 x 750 millilitres bottles of wine
    - 1 x 750 millilitres bottle of spirits.

It is also prohibited to sell port, wine in a glass container larger than one litre, or beer in bottles of 750 millilitres or more.

This is in the context that Tennant Creek has long suffered from social issues related to high rates of alcohol consumption. The residents have the strictest alcohol restrictions in the country to curb increasing criminal offences when offenders are intoxicated.

We take it for granted that we can just buy alcohol whenever we want. It is a big reality check to be confronted with those constraints. We did not buy any alcohol in Tennant Creek. But we did walk into a liquor shop in Katherine with the intention to restock our wine supplies. We were welcomed by a policeman in uniform at the door using an iPad linked to police databases.

We had to provide our drivers' licenses and were asked personal questions such as:

- 'Where do you intend to drink your purchases?' You must provide your accommodation address.
- 'Who do you intend to drink it with?' Just each other was the answer, but it was unnerving to reply to that question.

I felt like we were in the Inquisition. I understand on a rational level why they have such draconian measures, but I am not convinced it is the right way to improve the situation. Does it really change anything except make tourists feel nervous? But wait, it gets worse.

In Fitzroy Crossing (WA), we had a quick look at the Old Fitzroy Crossing Inn. It is a nice building by the Fitzroy River. We were told by the manager that anybody entering the pub must complete an alcohol breath test before being allowed in. If they have a reading higher than 0.05, they cannot enter. Chris asked if they were tested on exiting and the reply was 'No'. Chris asked how that made sense. The manager shrugged his shoulders and said he did not make the rules; the state government did. He had to abide by them, or he could risk losing his liquor license. We did not go in as it was only 11 am, but even then, there was zero appeal to go into such an establishment. In fact, we could not get out of the place quick enough. This is the ugly part of Australia that nobody talks about.

Other types of policing

Travelling around Australia was also an opportunity for pests, diseases, and weeds to travel with us as we visited different parts of the country. Crossing state lines came with different restrictions on what we could carry with us to minimise biosecurity risks to the agricultural industries and environment. We could not ignore those rules as there are heavy on-the-spot fines for taking prohibited items across borders. And of course, we wanted to do the right thing.

The first time we came across these rules was when we went from the Northern Territory into Western Australia. We had been informed early enough that we could not bring in any fruit, vegetables, or honey in an open jar. So, we ate a *big* salad to use everything in the fridge before getting to the border. We finished the honey in a delicious salad dressing. At the border, an inspector came aboard to check our fridge and freezer for contraband. Ours passed with flying colours. Still, we could have hidden illicit material anywhere else in the Goose. It is a bit of a farce really.

After suffering the Alcohol Police and the Fruit and Veggies Police, we were stopped at the Overlander Roadhouse (WA) by the Fish Police! Well, that is what we called the Fisheries Officers who were doing checks on fishermen's catches nowhere near water such as lakes, dams or ocean. I am now certain that Australia is the most regulated country in the world.

There was more weird and wonderful stuff ahead.

Corrigin Dog Cemetery

We love dogs, but we felt a little unnerved when we discovered the Corrigin Dog Cemetery by pure chance, as we were driving past. What attracted our attention was the proud dog statue at the entrance. Located 235 kilometres south-east of Perth, it has become one of Australia's most unique memorials and emerging tourist attractions. Rows of graves are loving reminders of where more than 200 dogs from across the country have been laid to rest.

The cemetery began in 1974 when local man Paddy Wright searched for a place to bury his beloved dog Strike. The Shire of Corrigin sent him to the sandy hill 5 kilometres west of town along Brookton Highway. It's a small town, so locals noticed it and a few others decided they would bury their dogs there too. Before they knew it, 20-odd dogs were buried, and a bit of a cemetery was happening. By the 1980s, Alan Henderson began putting headstones on the graves for the fee of a bag of cement.

Then in 1992, the monument was added, placing the dog by the side of the highway to honour man's best friend. That is when the tourist buses started pulling over just like we did. The dog cemetery wasn't put there as a tourist attraction, but it became one. We took time to read the tombstones and the stories of much-loved pets. We shed a tear remembering our own dogs that had passed.

The town of Corrigin further established its name into the history of human-dog relations in 2002 when it set a record by bringing together 1,527 dogs at the 'Dog in a Ute' event. The record still stands. People come from everywhere to attend the festival, which sounds like a lot of fun. However, it is a logistical nightmare to organise and is not held annually.

Gnomesville

The lady at the local information centre recommended we go visit Gnomesville in Wellington Mill (WA). But we felt it was not our kind of thing. I don't care for gnomes and never understood people collecting them and putting them in gardens. So, we dismissed it without another thought. But once again, inadvertently, we came to an intersection on the road, and I saw thousands of gnomes on the right side. It could not be ignored; we had to go see.

Gnomesville is one of those places that has been discussed all over the world. The proof is there to see; people send gnomes from everywhere. To us, they are a joke but there is obviously something peculiar about these small garden ornaments.

Nobody knows exactly how Gnomesville started, but it has grown exponentially over the years. It is estimated that there are now over 10,000 different gnomes in residence. The area has become a massive tourist attraction. We saw gnomes fishing, playing cricket, in rock bands, riding motorcycles and wearing face masks (very topical). They came in all sizes, shapes and colours. We were amazed to see gnomes from New York, England, Ireland and Spain. People bequeath them in their wills.

Unfortunately, in 2018 many of the gnomes were tragically washed away in a huge flood. So, the collection is rather messy in some sections. The natural area itself is pretty with a clear, crisp creek and lovely trees all around. The overall impression is that it needs a good clean up, but still the gnomes keep coming.

CHAPTER 20

Is that another national park?

I NEVER KNEW THERE WERE so many national parks in Australia until we literally kept driving straight from one to another. I looked it into it more deeply. Nearly 100 countries have lands classified as a national park (NP), which are used as conservation areas of a minimum size of 1,000 hectares. The United States started the ball rolling with Yellowstone in 1872. Big countries have many national parks. For example, there are 61 in the USA, 11 in China, 116 in India, 48 in Russia, 72 in Brazil and 47 in Canada.

They are called national parks because they are generally administered by a national government. But in Australia, that is not the case except for 6 true national parks. The other **675** parks are strangely enough run by state governments as they predate the federation of Australia. The first one established was the Royal National Park near Sydney in 1879.

Queensland leads the way with 237 national parks, closely followed by New South Wales with 235. Then comes Western Australia with 101, Victoria with 45, South Australia and Tasmania with 19 each, the Northern Territory with 24 and the Australian Capital Territory with just one. In addition, there are thousands of conservation areas, forest reserves and Indigenous protected areas.

Some people say that Australia has too many and we have to agree. Look at the numbers above for comparison's sake. Australia is smaller in size than most of the countries listed, yet we have up to 60 times more national parks. The mind boggles.

Nevertheless, visiting national parks is an inspiring experience and good for the soul. We were limited in our choices due to travelling with Watson. We hand-picked the ones we wanted to explore and hired dog sitters for the day.

We only spent a few weeks in our home state of Queensland and did not stop at any of its national parks because we knew we could always visit them later. Our goal was to go north as quickly as possible.

Northern Territory

1. Elsey NP

In the Northern Territory, we ended up staying 3 days near Elsey NP. The main attraction for us was Bitter Springs in the Katherine region. From the camping site there is a short 500-metre walk to the springs. These crystal-clear, slightly blue spring-fed thermal pools are set amongst palms and tropical woodlands. We saw people using pool noodles to float down with the current. We tried drifting down without any, but it was a battle to stay afloat. The current is quite strong. We bought two pool noodles in a shop at a crazy price and never looked back. It was paradise. We left Watson for a few hours at a time in the air-conditioned Goose while we bathed in the soothing waters. We had originally booked for one night, but we kept extending as it was too nice to depart.

2. Nitmiluk NP

Previously known at Katherine Gorge NP, Nitmiluk NP is a 13-gorge system that meanders around the Katherine River. We already mentioned that we took the 2-gorge cruise, and that was magnificent by itself. But we also did the walk to the top of the cliffs to see the river from above. It has awe-inspiring views from all angles, and it is worth spending at least a day there.

Eventually, we dragged ourselves away from the Northern Territory as Western Australia was calling.

Western Australia

1. Francois Perron NP, NINGALOO REEF NP AND Cape Range NP

We sneaked into FRANCOIS PERRON NP just to soak in the hot water tub. We then swam in NINGALOO REEF NP and floated over a whale shark in the waters below. The next day we drove around Cape Range NP and were impressed with the vistas overlooking Ningaloo Reef. We did a few hikes that were quite demanding but certainly worth the effort.

2. MILLSTREAM-CHICHESTER RANGE NP

We took one day to explore MILLSTREAM-CHICHESTER RANGE NP. THERE we had a refreshing swim in Python Pool against a magnificent backdrop of jagged ochre cliffs around us. We also had one of the best spots of the whole trip for lunch, with stunning views over the valley and the marvellous escarpments in the distance.

THE MAGICAL JOURNEY

3. KALBARRI NP

I had heard of the wildflowers of Western Australia. There are tours promoted on the east coast every springtime just to go see them. We arrived near the end of the season when many of the flowers had already wilted, but we were still mesmerised by the colourful spectacle of flowers by the side of the road and in the parks. I can only imagine how much more spectacular they are in full bloom.

Kalbarri NP is unique as it is divided into two sections: the coastal area and the inland area. We spent a whole day in the inland park. There is so much to see and do. The Murchison River has carved deep gorges with rock formations as old as 400 million years. The roads are sealed, and we went to all the lookouts and did all the short walks:

- Hawk's Head
- Ross Graham
- Z-Bend
- Skywalk
- The Loop
- Nature's Window

It is a photographer's paradise, and I went a little crazy with the camera. No wonder it is one of the most popular parks in Australia.

The coastal area was much smaller but also spectacular. We drove around it in a few hours the next day, stopping here and there to admire the cliffs over the Indian Ocean.

4.   Nambug NP

It is easy to see why Nambug NP is such an admired destination. Located 200 kilometres north of Perth, I consider it one of the most extraordinary places on Earth. The park contains the Pinnacles Desert from which you can see the Indian Ocean. It is where the desert meets the sea. The Pinnacles are limestone structures formed 30,000 years ago after the sea retreated and left behind deposits of seashells. Over time, the coastal winds blew away the surrounding sands, leaving the pillars exposed to the elements. Some can be as high as 3.5 metres.

There is a vehicle length limit due to the pillars being so close together. Getting between them with a longer vehicle requires some driving precision. Caravans are banned, but they can be safely disconnected and stored at the park entry.

It felt like we had landed on the moon. Some pinnacles are jagged, sharp-edged columns, rising to a point. Some are mushroom-like while others resemble tombstones. There are thousands dotted here and there on bright yellow sand. It is an experience not to be missed. Driving around the 4.5-kilometre trail is surreal.

My girlfriends in Brisbane had made me a special hand-painted tablecloth and had dared me to do a Priscilla Queen of the Desert impersonation, standing on top of the bus. This place was the perfect spot to attempt such a stunt. Climbing out of the window and precariously making my way on the top of the Golden Goose was a nerve-wrecking challenge. But I did it and Chris took the prize-winning photo. Not quite in the league of Priscilla as the bus was stationary, but terrifying enough for me!

THE MAGICAL JOURNEY

5.   Walpole-Nornalup NP

Walpole-Nornalup NP is home to the Valley of the Giants Tree Top Walk. This 40-metre-high walk suspended in the tops of the tingle trees is not for the faint-hearted. You can feel it shake with each step, but it is so picturesque up there. How often can you freely walk on top of trees?

6.   Torndirrup NP

Torndirrup NP has several natural wonders created by the wind and the pounding waves of the Southern Ocean. The views from the state-of-the-art platforms at The Gap and Natural Bridge are something else. This area also has a long whaling history and a trip to the whaling museum in town at the old whaling station was interesting, albeit very sad. To think we almost lost all the whales to relentless hunting…

IS THAT ANOTHER NATIONAL PARK?

7. STERLING RANGE NP

We spotted the Sterling Range NP for the first time as we followed the northern side heading east. We found one of our favourite camping sites by the side of the road in a roadwork gravel pit, which was much better than it sounds. We were all alone in the presence of those majestic mountains. We saw the sun setting over the range as we enjoyed happy hour and cooked a great dinner. We often remind ourselves of that beautiful, isolated spot with incredible views.

8. Porongurup NP

Porongurup NP protects one of the oldest mountain ranges in the world, formed by the collision of Australia and Antarctica over 1.2 billion years ago. A highlight is a 558-metre hike to the top of Castle Rock on the Granite Skywalk. We had drooled over the photos in the tourist brochures, and we just had to do it. It was a difficult climb and very challenging. We scrambled over rocks, through a tight crevice on steel loops inserted in the rock, up a ladder then along a catwalk to the summit with massive drops underneath. But once on top, we were captivated by the views north to the Stirling Range and south towards farmland and the ocean. Wow! Note: if you don't have a head for heights this place is not for you.

9. Tuart Forest NP

Tuart Forest NP is a peaceful forest woodland, and driving through it is a fantastic experience. It has the tallest and largest specimens of tuart trees, growing to more than 33 metres high and 10 metres in girth. Tuarts only grow on coastal limestone, 200 kilometres on either side of Perth. Tuart forests were once abundant, but Europeans cleared them for settlement, timber and fuel. Timber cutting operations continued into the twentieth century. Finally, the national park was declared in 1987. Now the area is protecting these majestic trees, well-known for their height and straightness.

10. Leeuwin-Nationaliste NP

Leeuwin-Nationaliste NP is named after the locations at either end of the park: Cape Leeuwin and Cape Naturaliste. It is the most visited national park in Western Australia. It is no wonder since this is where Mother Nature decided to show off all her wares. It has surf beaches, forests, rugged coastlines and 100 limestone caves. We walked to the top of Cape Leeuwin lighthouse to witness where the Indian Ocean and the Southern Ocean meet. It was not like the photos we had seen with a visible line in the water and different colours on either side. It was disappointing to tell the truth. I had so looked forward to seeing that place. But it does not always look like the brochure, depending on the weather and time of the day.

Over one big day, we explored three of the four cave systems opened for tourists. Lake Cave has a series of stairways and paths that descend through a large crater with huge karri trees growing from its depths. The cave's lake never dries up and offers stunning reflections from the path that runs along its edge. A prominent feature is the Suspended Table, a large flat area of flowstone supported just above the lake from above by two large columns. It looks like it is floating in the air: a mesmerising optical illusion.

Mammoth Cave features an outstanding formation that looks like a large, coloured shawl. It is also home to the largest megafauna (large extinct marsupials) fossil deposits in Australia. Ten thousand specimens were recovered by the Western Australia Museum in the early 1990s. The jawbone of an extinct marsupial about the size of a cow is visible in the wall of this cavern.

Jewel Cave is the largest show cave in Western Australia with three immense chambers. We were awed by the scale of the first chamber, which contains one of the longest straw stalactites found in any tourist cave in Australia. Nature's finest and most meticulous lace work. It left us speechless.

11. Gloucester NP

Gloucester NP is famous for the journey through the majestic karri forest. Karri trees only grow in southwestern Australia and can reach 95 metres. Western Australia's most famous climbing karri tree is the Gloucester Tree, which was once a fire lookout tree. Daring people used to climb up the 153 pegs without any safety guards. I might have tried but it was closed due to safety issues.

12. Wellington NP

Wellington NP is a must-stop place to visit for one good reason. It is where you can see King Jarrah, a tree estimated to be between 300 and 500 years old. The tree stands 36 metres high. It has survived Mother Nature's worst treatments in the form of bush fires, storms, lightning and insect attacks. A boardwalk and viewing platform enable you to get as close as possible to this superb old tree.

South Australia

We visited four national parks in this state. The main one was inevitable as we crossed the Nullarbor.

1. Nullarbor NP

Nullarbor NP has the world's largest semi-arid karst (cave) landscapes. Most of the park's landscape is flat except where the surface has collapsed into sinkholes, revealing large underground caverns. We did not stop to visit the sinkholes as we had Watson with us.

Where the barren landscape meets the Southern Ocean are the longest sea cliffs in the world: the 100-kilometres-long Bunda Cliffs. We camped right on the edge of the cliffs, on the mainland side of a suspiciously large crack in the rock that was parallel to the cliff face. We marvelled at the beauty of it all. Our immediate view spanned the rugged coastline, which made for an unforgettable sunset. We felt unparalleled serenity and gratitude just to be there.

2. Ikara-Flinders Ranges NP

We were keen to see the iconic park Ikara-Flinders Ranges NP, but it was getting too hot to comfortably enjoy it. The best we could do was camp near the southern edge and admire the mountains from afar. We are definitely going back one day to get up close and personal with the towering clifftops and deep craters including Wilpena Pound–a gigantic natural amphitheatre encompassing the Flinders Ranges' highest point, St Mary Peak.

3. Coffin Bay NP

Coffin Bay NP has a wonderful, sealed road section we enjoyed driving around. We travelled to Point Avoid (we could not avoid it) and Golden Island where we were rewarded with spectacular views and endless beaches over the bluest blue waters.

4. Murray River NP

Murray River NP is all about the mighty 130-million-year-old river that is steeped in rich Aboriginal history, culture and heritage. It is 2,500 kilometres long, flowing through New South Wales and Victoria then into South Australia. It is the third largest navigable river in the world. We followed it through two states. Even though I had spent 11 months working on the Murray River in 1993 on a cruise ship, I realised I had not seen much of it after all. There were some amazing lookouts and pit stops along the way. It was still recovering from the terrible floods when we visited, and piles of mud and temporary levee banks were everywhere. It did not deter us, and we were very happy to be exploring it at our pace.

Victoria

We crossed over to Victoria. We aimed to continue following the Murray River, but on the way, we were compelled to stop and go up Mount Abrupt in the Grampians NP.

1. Grampians NP

From the road, Mount Abrupt's sheer rocky cliffs are an impressive sight at 823 metres high. We seriously wondered if we should tackle the challenging hike to the top. It is a 6.3-kilometre, grade-3 walk with a recommended time of 2.5 hours to complete it. But it was not as bad as we anticipated. There were lots of steep steps to the summit, but also flatter sections. They were good spots to catch our breath and take in the dramatic scenery. Once we got to the top, there was a metal tripod on the rocks. Maybe a surveyor's marker. It was a weird thing to find at that height.

THE MAGICAL JOURNEY

We finally crossed into New South Wales.

New South Wales

1. Blue Mountains NP

Blue Mountains NP, where I have bushwalked several times, never ceases to surprise me. This World Heritage-listed Park is home to the famous Three Sisters and iconic lookouts over plunging waterfalls. The lookouts and the cable car ride are a tourist must if time is short. The whole park is full of such beauty that you need quite a bit of time to appreciate it all via the lookouts and walks. We really needed more time to explore all its hidden treasures. But we were on a tight schedule to get to our housesit in North Sydney.

2. Kuringai Chase NP

Kuringai Chase NP protects a major part of Northern Sydney's waterways, including the Hawkesbury River, Pittwater and Cowan Water. The best views are from Barrenjoey Lighthouse. I am familiar with this park, having worked for 5 years on cruise ships on the Hawkesbury River. It holds a special place in my heart and always will. The funny part is that when I was young, I used to watch the television program *Skippy*, which was filmed in this park. Is anyone old enough to remember that iconic program, which put Australia on the world map? I watched a dubbed French version. I never imagined in my wildest dreams that one day I would live and work in this area.

3.   Myall Lake NP

Myall Lake NP is located north of Newcastle. We drove through it following the coast, soaking up the scenery combining RAMSAR listed wetlands, trees, ocean beaches and lighthouses. An added bonus was taking the unexpected little vehicular ferry at Bombah Point to cross the lake. It was so small that we were astonished that it could take the bus and other vehicles at the same time.

4.   Dorrigo NP

Dorrigo NP is part of the Gondwana Rainforests of Australia World Heritage Area and offers superb scenery that's been millions of years in the making. For me it was all about the waterfalls on the 185-kilometre scenic drive, Waterfall Way. It is a special place. An elevated walk gives views from the forest to the sea. Wollomombi Falls are the second tallest falls in Australia where the river plummets 220 metres into the valley below. We did not see it in full flood and yet it was still remarkable.

5.   Warrumbungle NP

Warrumbungle NP is Australia's first Dark Sky Park as mentioned in a previous chapter. That is definitely a good reason to visit. But it has much more to offer. It was created over millions of years from an extinct shield volcano. The mountains are jagged; one is even called 'The Breadknife'. You don't have to have much of an imagination to identify that one. The Warrumbungles rise sharply from ridges dotted with eucalypts on the surrounding plains. We did the short walk from the carpark to the Whitegum lookout and were rewarded with outstanding views.

6. Yuraygir NP

Yuraygir NP has a beautiful 65-kilometre coastal walk along a series of tracks, trails, beaches, and a rock platform. We only undertook a small section, but that was enough to wet our appetite to return one day and do the whole track. Even on our short walk, the changing scenery was gobsmacking.

CHAPTER 21

Is that really art?

AUSTRALIA IS BLESSED WITH AN infinity of artists, some better than others without a doubt. We were flabbergasted by the amount of creativity demonstrated everywhere we went. You can find any size, any shape, any material. Some creations were quizzical, but most were moving. I know that I am easily impressed, but I found plenty of things to admire. I could write a whole book just on the art we encountered on our magical journey.

The vineyards

Many vineyards have their own sculpture park in their gardens. When money is of no concern, some extraordinary pieces can be added to their wealthy owners' collection. Once we were lucky to be in the right place at the right time.

Nothing prepared us for the surprise of the **Salvador Dali** collection at D'Arenberg Winery (SA). There were huge sculptures on the grounds and smaller sculptures inside. They were limited edition reproductions with hefty price tags, some heading towards $2 million. I did fall in love with a couple of them, but our budget could not allow for such expenses.

THE MAGICAL JOURNEY

Since 1989, those 25 monumental sculptures valued at $20 million have been displayed in cities such as Rome, London, Beijing and Singapore. And there they were near Adelaide! The exhibition is a true celebration of Dali's creative genius.

Now, while Dali was impressive, British and Australian artists **Gillie and Marc** are something else. They are 'the most successful and prolific creators of public art in New York's History' according to the New York Times. Their innovative sculptures are redefining what public art should be. We discovered them, having never heard of them before, in Onslow (WA) with the Paparazzi sculptures. Then they kept popping up in strange places: the life-size Lobster Fisherman in Port Macdonell (SA) and the anatomically correct human/dog sculptures in a tiny winery called Gundog Estate in Pokolbin (NSW). I absolutely love their work.

Renowned bush artists

John Murray in Lightning Ridge (NSW) is a realist painter who works with acrylic. His paintings are like whimsical pictures of the outback. His art mixes desert landscapes with human folly and quirky animals, most notably adorable emus. His art is everywhere

IS THAT REALLY ART?

in the town itself, and on the outskirt stands Stanley the Emu by the side of the road. He is 15 metres high and has been made out of four Volkswagen beetles' carcasses. It is classic outback whimsy stuff, and he has been welcoming visitors there since 2013. Walking into John's gallery is like walking into a playful world. His paintings, which are a bit lowbrow for some city art afficionados, brought a smile to my face. I could have bought so many.

Mark Norval in Derby (WA) is an internationally acclaimed artist who uses different media. He paints, he prints, he sketches, he sculpts, he writes, and he organises music events. I am not sure if he sleeps! He has giant sculptures on the salt lakes outside of town. He is also totally involved in the local Indigenous art scene, fostering budding Aboriginal artists, and dedicating the back of his gallery to them. When we visited, there were three Indigenous painters at work on the big tables (see Chapter 31).

The gallery showcases Mark's creations and the artwork of many Aboriginal artists from the Kimberley region of Western Australia. The place is packed wall to wall. Moreover, there is Australia's best historical carved Boab Nut display and an extensive collection of rare and beautiful seashells. For the music fans there is a collection of 5,000 of the best LPs ever recorded. The gallery is closed during November, December and January. Thank goodness we were there in the right season. I would not have wanted to miss that place.

Malcolm Craig in Kapunda (SA) came to our attention as we walked into Kapunda Community Gallery. So much talent in such a small place. Malcom was one of the main artists exhibiting there. He uses different media in his paintings and sculptures, such as pastels, timber, chicken wire and scrap metal. He has even done some paintings using vegemite, which comes out a sort of sepia colour. Malcom's inspiration is Australian wildlife. His art is displayed everywhere in town, starting with a sculpture of a man sitting on the bench right outside the gallery. He also works in a second-hand bookshop down the street where Chris went in to have a chat with him. I missed out on meeting the man as I stayed outside with Watson. But the result was that Chris secretly commissioned a unique sculpture of wrens drinking from a tap, which was presented to me months later for our anniversary. It now sits proudly amongst our bird collection in our house.

Street art

There is a surprising amount of street and park art everywhere. Just walking around the main streets looking at shopfront windows, we came across so many creative murals on the sides of buildings.

THE MAGICAL JOURNEY

You can even find art in the middle of roundabouts. I loved the tin camels in Norseman (WA).

We found sculpture trails in the most remote areas. The Utes in the Paddock on a 25-acre block in Condobolin (NSW) is one example. We made a detour specifically to see this unique attraction. The Utes in the Paddock was a concept created by Jana and Graham Pickles in 2015. The Lachlan Shire Council has come onboard and is dedicating time, energy, and marketing resources to further develop and promote this outdoor gallery. A large tourist centre is being completed next to the extensive ute display, and it is also going to house an indoor art gallery. Some of the locals reckon that it's a waste of money. While we were there the utes display was attracting a continuous stream of visitors. I think the Council is smart.

IS THAT REALLY ART?

Recycling art

We commend the trend in recycling materials and turning them into fine works of art. Some are made entirely of old rusty farming equipment parts and tools. The ingenuity demonstrated in creating such magnificent pieces out of what could be declared 'junk' is indescribable. Masterpieces in our eyes. People are so imaginative! How does someone turn motorcycle fuel tanks into baby emus?

Who turns old bits of metals into cows and puts them on top of a supermarket roof? I don't even know what made me look up there to see them. Maybe I felt I was being watched?

How did someone think of transforming old car bonnets into information signs to a point of interest?

Then there is the quirky sense of humour and creations that just catch your eye as you drive by. You make a U-turn to have a better look because you can't believe your eyes.

There is Elvis in the Salt Lake.

There is a boat, a fisherman and a fish on the side of the road.

There are countless weird and wonderful musical instruments such as this one:

We walked into an op shop and were informed we could step into another dimension if we were brave enough. This is what confronted us. Did somebody indulge in too much wacky tabaccy?

IS THAT REALLY ART?

The big art

On a gigantic scale, nothing beats the wall of **Wellington Dam** in Western Australia. It is the largest dam mural painting in the world. Painted by Australian artist Guido Van Helten in 2021, the sheer size of it is mind blowing. It covers 8,000 square metres of the 34-metre-high by 367-metre-wide wall. It took four months of relentless work to finish the masterpiece. The artwork is called 'Reflections' and is inspired by local stories and photos. It is an emotional piece to see from the lookout dangling over the Collie River. I was close to tears and the photo does not do it justice.

We loved the huge **painted silos and water towers**. The Australian silo art trail is a gem, and you can find more information at *https://www.australiansiloarttrail.com/*. It all started in Northam, Western Australia in 2015 as a clever way to attract visitors to regional areas. For some communities, it has proven to be a lifeline. There are now 61 silo art sites in all states, and more are being added. We found some accidentally, but we often went looking for them as well.

Standing in front of those tall silos (up to 90 metres high) with their detailed paintings was breathtaking. They make such an impact. I am in total admiration of the work involved in painting on such a demanding canvas. I wish I had one artistic bone in my body to create such beauty.

THE MAGICAL JOURNEY

Some of the silos offer a canvas for nighttime sight-and-sound shows. It appears a few councils are finding this a cheaper alternative to painting a silo. I suppose it also offers variety as the shows can change with the seasons. This is one of those shows at sunset:

On a different level of 'big art' is the unique art gallery we found 12 metres underground in Lightning Ridge (NSW). The **Chambers of the Black Hand** started in 1997. English born Ron Canlin started mining black opals in 1982. But he was spending more money than he was making. Instead of giving up, Ron decided to turn his mine into a tourist attraction. He dug by hand 112 stairs, 18 metres deep, from the surface down to the opal clay level, so visitors could get an authentic and unforgettable experience.

Fifteen years after opening the mine, Ron started carving the soft sandstone walls out of boredom. He is totally self-taught. He carved using nothing but a butter knife. You read that right–a *butter knife!*

He is in his eighties and officially retired now, but he still does a little carving. There are 900 carvings in the 26 chambers that he has created. This is a one-of-a-kind, not-to-be-missed experience and I still can't believe what I saw. Donning miners' hats, we walked from an Australiana Chamber with koalas and kangaroos onto an Egyptian chamber filled with humorous hieroglyphics and a replica of an Egyptian tomb. After that, we turned around the corner and found not one but four Buddhas that were 5 metres tall! We continued through to the African wildlife section. There, climbing to the ceiling and walls we saw well-known superheroes, followed by some famous faces and a dedicated space to under the sea creatures. It is easy to see how much Ron's skills have developed over the years. In the most recent chambers, he has added colours, and his sculptures are more finely chiselled.

IS THAT REALLY ART?

Christmas art

Christmas seems to be a catalyst for ingenuity and fun, particularly in the bush. We drove along a country road for dozens of kilometres and stopped every five minutes to take photos of the most original Christmas decorations we had ever seen. Most featured bales of hay and Santa in various states of sobriety. We just loved how the farmers were in competition with each other as to who could produce the most outrageous decorations.

From the ridiculous to the sublime, Mandurah in Western Australia took Christmas decorations to an upper level of sophistication. I had never seen such shiny things in broad daylight. I can only imagine what they looked like at night. Unfortunately, we did not make it to the evening show. Nevertheless, the artsy Christmas display on the estuary foreshores was astounding. Chris even enjoyed a ride on the fancy trike, naturally.

Town art

Some towns go out of their way to be different and attract tourists. Sometimes the whole town gets into the action. It is not just one artist running with enthusiasm, but the whole community gets behind the idea. Two towns in particular come to mind.

We were driving back from visiting the mind-blowing Wave Rock when we stopped in **Hyden (WA)**. The local artists there have put so much time and effort in developing a sculpture park like no other. The sculptures are all made from scrap iron and tell the history of the town and its most interesting local residents. It is fascinating to walk down the line of artworks and read the humorous signs. There is a sense of fun, community and belonging in that place.

We also made a special trip to see **Walcha (NSW)**. It had been recommended as a 'must see' place by friends due to its unique motorcycle-themed café. The Walcha Royal Café is an Art Deco building with quirky sculptures made from recycled motorcycle parts. But once we got there, we found there was so much more to see.

Walcha boasts the Open-Air Gallery where local, national, and international artists have created a unique streetscape with about 41 sculptures and artworks, plus 30 sculptured veranda posts (a novel idea) in front of the local businesses. Supposedly there is about one artwork per every 85 citizens, making Walcha quite a cultural and artistic community for its size. It was worth making a detour for.

CHAPTER 22

How did we miss that?

THE MAGICAL JOURNEY IS ALL about what we saw on our lap of Australia. We could write a travel guide about all the things we *missed seeing* for one reason or another. And we could travel a whole new lap of Australia in the reverse direction to tick most of those boxes off. The reasons why we missed some attractions range from the ridiculous to the realistic, and some are pretty funny. Here are the things we missed, grouped together under the reasons why we missed them.

Wrong season

It never occurred to us to check beforehand if there were specific things that we definitely wanted to see and when it was possible to see them. Coddiwompling does not include that kind of planning ahead. Therefore, we showed up either too early or too late to see the following attractions. You can see why we really need to go back to South Australia.

- Gathering of the orcas in Brehmer Bay (WA)–from January to April

- Southern Right whales giving birth at Head of Bight (SA)–from mid-May to late October
- Giant Cuttle fish in Whyalla (SA)–June and July
- The Old Steam Train ride in Pichi Richi (SA)–from March to November
- Argadell's station (SA)–closed in summer
- Yalumba cooperage live tour in Angaston (SA)–available when grape harvest is on from January to March
- Pink Lake in Meningie (SA)–pink only in January and February
- MacKenzie Falls (VIC)–even though they flow all year-round there is not much water during summer, supposedly spectacular viewing in wintertime

Wrong day

It was frustrating to find that many tourist attractions were only open on some days and within certain hours with a minuscule window of opportunity. We understand that many are manned by volunteers who are getting older and less available. Therefore, there were many disappointments along the way:

- Bunker Museum in Mallacoota (VIC)–open for two hours on Tuesday or Sunday
- Powerhouse Museum in Streaky Bay (WA)–open between 2 pm and 5 pm on Tuesday and Friday
- Two-Fold Bay cruise in Eden (NSW)–operates on Sunday during off season
- Staircase to the Moon, Cable Beach (WA)–between March and September on a clear full moon night. (In truth it can be viewed in many places at the right phase of the moon where there is a shallow shelving beach that provides considerable water reflection.)

Natural causes

It was difficult to comprehend the impact natural causes have on tourism until we saw how many things we missed out on because Mother Nature said so:

- Blow Hole and Whistling Rocks at Cape Baver (SA)–tide was not high enough to see the blow hole, nor hear the Whistling Rocks
- Hiring a houseboat in Renmark (SA)–Murray River floods meant no clearance under Paringa Bridge and nowhere to go with the houseboat
- Wombeyan Caves (NSW)–closed since October 2022 due to bush fires *and* floods!
- Wolgan Valley (NSW)–closed due to a landslide in November 2022
- Pink Lake in Esperance (WA)–has not been pink for 70 years!
- Evans Lookout in the Blue Mountains (NSW)–raining so hard that we could not see a thing

Signs

Oh, this is a tough one. Signs can be a godsend when they are accurate. Sometimes they are non-existent, or they have been removed by locals who don't want tourists there. Besides that, a lot of signs get souvenired and may not be replaced. Still others show signs of gunshots; the 'Os' seem irresistible to some trigger-happy gun owners. More often, the signs are misleading or at worse create a false sense of expectation of great things ahead. Here is a list to show you what I mean:

- The historic Old Nullarbor Roadhouse (WA): We did not know it was there until later when looking online. The new roadhouse is where we stopped to fill up. I am

sorry to have missed that when we were so close. There were simply no signs.
- Camels on the Nullarbor: We never saw one, even though there were signs to watch out for them.
- The end of the dog fence in South Australia: We never saw it because there were no signs.
- Painted Silo in Cowell (SA): We missed it because there were no signs and we only saw the white side of the silo (the back side). We wondered, if they had bothered to go to the trouble of getting it painted, why wouldn't they signpost it well?
- Stoney Creek trestle bridge in Nowa Nowa (VIC): The longest such bridge in Australia and with bad signage, we never found it.
- Mozart (NSW): No signs anywhere but it was on a map. I so wanted to visit this town with the cute name. It may just be a station name.

4WD access

We knew sometimes that we could not access certain areas because they were true 4WD tracks. We had forced the Golden Goose as far as she could go (see Chapter 9). Unfortunately, we had to turn around in some cases when it was obvious that we should not push our luck:

- Pink Lake in MacDonnell (SA): It was 60 kilometres of dirt road to get to that picture perfect pink lake so close to the blue ocean, but that was too much dirt road for us. It broke my heart to not see it.
- Lawn Hills and Adels Grove near Gregory Downs (QLD): We were warned to not attempt it as it was so bad even 4WDs had trouble getting there without getting a flat tyre.

- The heritage truss Monkerei Bridge in Stroud (NSW): To get there is a bitumen road that looks like a bad dirt road; pretty much 4WD only.
- Pokolbin Lookout (NSW): Strictly 4WD access.

Miscellaneous reasons

Following are all the weird and wonderful reasons why we missed out on seeing some things we really wanted to see. Sometimes we would have driven a long way for nothing. But on the other hand, occasionally we found a surprise while we were there. You can never tell which way it is going to go.

- Cape Levesque on Dampier Peninsula (WA): We found out that the resort was the only access point and it had been controversially closed down recently.
- Swimming in a shark cage in Port Lincoln (SA): The cost of $561 per person was a bigger deterrent than the fear of sharks!
- The whole of Tasmania: We really wanted to go, but the return ferry was booked out for March and April. Obviously seasoned travellers book ahead to get off the island before it gets too cold.
- Mango Winery in Mandurah (WA): I was keen to taste that mango wine, but the winery was closed for a private function the day we turned up.
- Mount Lofty café (SA): It was closed due to water being treated the day we visited.
- Hiring a go-cart at The Bend Motorsport Park in Tailem Bend (SA): A car drifting event was on. However, the awesome complex was open with a free viewing platform for drop-ins like us.
- The light and sound show in Wallaroo (SA): We saw the video on the big screen but without sound.
- The zig zag train in Lithgow (NSW): It was about to re-open after major renovations.

- Govett's Leap lookout, Blue Mountains (NSW): It was closed due to major upgrade works.
- Overnight stay at the Dubbo Zoo (NSW): The online booking system confirmed our booking only to be told it was not in the system when we arrived. Disappointing.
- Swinging Bridge in Canowindra (NSW): It was deemed unsafe in February 2023 and shut down, just 3 months before we arrived. Missed by that much!
- Mount Kaputar summit lookout (NSW): Motorhomes and caravans are not allowed up the hill, to our great disappointment.
- Gloucester Tree in Gloucester NP (WA): This spotter's tree, for bush fire detection, has been famous for decades as a heart-stopping climbing experience. It had finally been closed for safety reasons. It is just pegs in the tree trunk all the way to the spiralling top. However, for the brave at heart the nearby Bicentennial Tree in Warren NP is still open and available for climbing. We did not make it there.
- Seeing a thorny devil in Exmouth (WA): We never saw one even though we were told they were *everywhere*.
- Platypus in Ducal Creek (NSW): Locals said they were definitely there, but we never saw one. Maybe they saw us though!

PART 3

The Educational Journey

I am unashamedly a nerd. I always loved school and hated the summer holidays. I could not wait to get back to the classroom and learn some more interesting facts. My life has been filled with learning all kinds of subjects. I have an eclectic collection of interests: sailing, music, singing, dancing, geology, aromatherapy, remedial massage, dog behaviour, veterinary nursing, navigation, occupational therapy, and mental health to name a few.

The trip was a smorgasbord of lessons learned about what makes Australia tick. The knowledge accumulated covered so many different aspects of history, economy, geology, flora and fauna. My mind was filled up with facts and figures. I read and took photos of just about every single information sign that appeared in front of me. We visited many museums with more interesting facts to stow away. I cannot claim to remember everything I read and saw. Searches on the internet helped refresh my memory and fill in the gaps. It saved me going back through hundreds of tourist brochures. A word of warning: There are a lot of numbers ahead. You may want to gaze over them quickly if you don't care for statistics.

CHAPTER 23

Does history repeat?

IT IS ONLY AS I have matured that I have reflected on my own past and the past of others. I am not so sure that history never repeats as I have seen plenty of patterns recurring in my own lifetime.

My knowledge of Australian history was gathered in bits and pieces after I landed here in 1985. The first film I saw was *Breaker Morant*, which is a sombre way to be initiated into the colonial past. Of course, I was aware of Captain James Cook setting off on an exploration of the southern land and in 1770 'claiming' Terra Australia Incognita. I now know this was all very east-coast centric. Western Australia revealed a whole different side of history that I had never heard of. Maybe this is taught in Australian schools, but a refresher is never wasted.

Most people think of history as a boring subject, and so did I. It was not my favourite subject in school since it was all about remembering supposedly important dates to which I had no connection. But I have since changed my mind. A young man who was the skipper on our boat trip to Dirk Hartog Island introduced us in an engaging way to history. It is not all about dates but more about understanding how we got here today.

The First People

Let us acknowledge the First Nations of Australia who were definitely the first habitants of the Great Southern Land. The latest research states that they have been here for at least 65,000 years in some areas. There is more on that subject in Chapter 30. The question in this chapter is about who the first white fellas to inhabit Australia were. Scholars argue over who was the first non-Indigenous person to set foot on Australia and become the first 'resident'. It may have been Chinese or Portuguese sailors in the 1500's, but there is no solid evidence.

Dirk Hartog, a Dutchman, made a brief landing on an island off Western Australia's coast, now bearing his name, in 1616. He left a pewter dish on a tree with an inscription to prove it. Interestingly, 81 years later, Captain Willem de Vlamingh landed on that same island (what are the odds?) and discovered Hartog's pewter dish with the post rotted away. He removed it and replaced it with another plate, copying the inscription, which was attached to a new post. He took that original pewter dish back with him to The Netherlands. Australia's oldest maritime relic sits in the Rijksmuseum in Amsterdam.

But I digress. Back to who was here permanently first from foreign lands.

Apparently 10 years earlier than Hartog, another Dutchman Willem Janszoon had set foot on the mainland near Cape York. But he did not stay either. He is reportedly the first European to have had contact with Australian Aboriginals.

So, who were the first white people to settle here?

In 1629, the Batavia (more on that in the next chapter) struck a reef near Geraldton. The Batavia story and the many books about it are worth a read. As a result of a mutiny, the two youngest rebels, Wouter Loos and Jan Pelgrom, were punished by being left ashore with a boat and provisions. Nothing more was ever heard from them. There are indications that they survived and were taken in by the local Aboriginal tribes. Their punishment made them involuntarily the first recorded European residents of Australia. Researchers believe they may have had relationships with the local women. Studies investigating DNA testing have released early results confirming there is Western European, not English, DNA in some Western Australia Aboriginals. This could mean that Europeans settled in Australia long before its post-Captain-Cook colonial history began. This is big news and yet not many people know about it!

We looked everywhere for the commemorative plaque indicating where Loos and Pelgrom had landed. We found it in the most obscure place without any tourist signs of any kind. We were amazed that something as significant as this historical fact was so well hidden.

The shipwrecks

Before a single Englishman set foot on the east coast of Australia, hundreds of ships were sailing past the west coast. They were searching for oriental spices. We take spices for granted today and just pick the bottles up in the supermarkets. But in medieval Europe spices such as cloves, nutmeg, cinnamon, and pepper were scarce and extremely valuable. They were used in medicine to relieve pain. They preserved cooked food and added flavour to meat and alcoholic drinks. Last but not least, spices were deemed to be aphrodisiacs. The race was on to get those exotic/erotic spices from Asia to Europe as fast as possible, and every European country wanted a piece of the action.

The big name in that game was the United Dutch East India Company (from the Dutch: *Verenigde Oostindische Compagnie*), shortened to VOC. It started as a chartered company in 1602, merging existing companies into the first stock-based company in the world. It was granted a 21-year monopoly by the Dutch government to carry out trade activities in Asia. This was a super powerful company. It was so big that someone compared it to Google, Microsoft, Facebook, Apple, and Amazon all joined together. Imagine that amount of wealth knowing Jeff Bezos is the third richest man in the world with his Amazon empire.

There was nobody else who came close to VOC in the Asia trading route. It surpassed all its competitors. Between 1602 and 1796, the VOC sent nearly a million Europeans to work in the Asia trade on 4,785 ships. Their efforts landed more than two million tonnes of goods. The mind boggles at the scale of such buzzing activity.

It was all about the sailing ships back then. They were navigating the coast south from Europe, down the African continent on the west coast, past the Cape of Good Hope, on to the east coast of Africa, India and finally to what is now known as Indonesia.

Before the ships, since ancient times, everything came through the overland route known as the Silk Road. I have vague memories of that subject being taught at school. The Arab merchants introduced cloves to Europe around the second century and a raging trade began. Their monopoly on the overland route continued until 1497 when Portuguese explorer Vasco da Gama rounded the Cape of Good Hope and sailed to India. Suddenly there was a better way to move the spices to Europe. Portugal dominated the spice trade during the sixteenth century. It appears that the Portuguese even visited and mapped the Australian coast as early as 1522. But another nation was rising up to challenge them.

The Dutch were winning the race following the traditional sea routes, but time was money and faster routes were sought. A better route was discovered, the Brouwer route, going south into the Roaring Forties to pick up the fast winds. This rapid traverse of the Indian Ocean, which could save weeks of sailing, came with its own hazards. The ships had to turn northwards at the correct point. There was no radar or satellite communications that make navigation so exact today. Back then navigation was done by 'dead reckoning' based on roughly estimated speed during the southerly traverse of the Indian Ocean. The decision to turn north was based on the captain's judgement. If they turned too early, that was an inconvenience. If they turned much too late, they became wind-locked to the south of Australia and the voyage failed. However, if they turned *just* too late, often the ships would find themselves driven dangerously close to the western coast of Australia, which was fraught with disaster. The rugged coast was unforgiving for wooden sailing ships, with many shallow reefs to get stuck on. There are over 1,600 sunken ships off the western coast of Australia. We followed the Shipwreck Trail for hundreds of kilometres. The most famous of which is the *Batavia*.

Batavia

In 1628, the VOC built in Amsterdam the largest ship ever constructed at that time, the *Batavia*. It was on its maiden voyage to Indonesia, filled with treasures such as silver and gold coins. A mutiny was fomenting but the ship sank first. It hit a reef in the Abrolhos, 60 kilometres off the coast near Geraldton (WA). There were 340 people onboard. At least 100 people died in the aftermath of the wreck. But over 200 crew and passengers made it to an island. The commander and some crew took a 10-metre longboat to the city of Batavia (now Jakarta) looking for help. An incredible endurance journey of 3,000 kilometres followed.

When they returned two months later to rescue the survivors, a mutiny had finally taken place. They learned of the massacre of over 125 men, women and children. It was the lowest of the lowest acts of barbarism and brutality. This tragic story is still Australia's greatest mass murder. The culprits were found and severely punished. Their right hands were cut off before being hanged at the gallows. Two mutineers were saved that ordeal but were marooned on the mainland instead (see previous chapter).

The wreck of the *Batavia* was found in 1963 along with most of the gold and silver coins. To me, the most impressive things they recovered were the 137 stones used as ballast. They were meant to be a grand portico for a VOC castle to be built in Jakarta. It is now standing proudly in the Geraldton Maritime Museum after the stones sat on the ocean floor for over 300 years. It is amazing to see! The replica of the longboat sitting in the harbour near the museum is also an eye opener. To realise how small that boat was to succeed in that rescue journey to Jakarta showed us how tough and resilient sailors were back then.

More relics, including parts of the hull, have been relocated to the Shipwreck Museum in Freemantle. By that stage of our travels, we were a bit over shipwrecks and did not visit that museum. Maybe that was a mistake, and we should have gone in to have a look.

Batavia was not the only VOC ship to come unstuck near Geraldton in Western Australia.

Zuytdorp and Zeewijk

On the 1st August 1711, *Zuytdorp* was dispatched bearing a load of freshly minted silver coins. Like other trading ships she travelled the Brouwer Route, using the strong Roaring Forties winds to carry her across the Indian Ocean to within sight of the west coast of Australia (then called New Holland), whence she would have turned north towards Batavia. *Zuytdorp* didn't arrive at her destination and was never heard from again. It is believed that she was shipwrecked off Western Australia coast and that survivors were helped by local Aboriginals.

Tamala Station (located between Kalbarri and Shark Bay) head stockman Tom Pepper reported finding a wreck to the authorities in 1941. It took 13 years for the Western Australian

Museum staff to investigate the possible recovery of the silver coins. Later, in the eighties, a multi-disciplinary team attended the wreck and recovered many artefacts. Incredibly, one was a glass beaker found in a rocky niche. It survived there undamaged for over 250 years. The diver who found it was equally surprised. What a find! I felt so privileged to admire it in the Museum. I have a thing for glassware.

The *Zeewijk* was another VOC ship. She set off on her maiden voyage to Batavia in November 1726 with 10 chests full of silver coins. She hit a reef on 9th of June 1727, near where the *Batavia* had sunk almost 100 years earlier. But she did not sink right away. The ship remained virtually intact on the reef platform for a few months, enabling survivors to get ashore, camp on what was later named Gun Island and recover a great deal of material from the wreck. A rescue group of 11 of the fittest survivors and the First Mate were chosen to set off for Batavia in the longboat. Sounds familiar? They never made it and disappeared without a trace.

The survivors were left to their own devices and had lost hope of being rescued. They decided to build a second ship they called the *Sloepie*. They used timbers from the wreck and mangrove trees found on nearby islands. They also equipped her with two swivel mounted cannons (from the *Zeewijk*) to protect the treasure from pirates. Consequently, she was the first European ship to be built in Australian waters. Finally, 82 out of the initial crew of 208 sailed the 20-metre-long sloop to reach Batavia one month later on 30th April 1728. That is one incredible tale of survival and determination.

The shipwreck was found in 1968 by divers. Many objects were found near the wreck site, which are now in the Western Australian Museum. There are also some items in the Maritime Museum in Geraldton.

In June 2012, a commemorative plaque was unveiled in Kalbarri for the 300th anniversary of *Zuytdorp's* wreck. It also mentions the *Batavia* and the *Zeewijk*. We saw that plaque and reflected on the thousands of poor souls lost on the rugged west coast of Australia over the centuries.

However, not all wrecks were due to the jagged coastline. Some were due to human intervention during the Second World War.

HMAS Sydney II and HSK Kormoran

We saw so many memorials dedicated to the historical and dreadful battle between HMAS *Sydney II* and *HSK Kormoran*. I was wondering what the fascination was all about because I am not really into war history. But it dawned on me eventually what a significant human loss it had been for two countries at war: Australia and Germany.

On the 19th of November 1941, the Australian light cruiser *HMAS Sydney II* and the German raider *Kormoran* (disguised as a merchant ship) engaged in a battle off the coast of Western Australia. The encounter lasted *only 30 minutes*, and in that short time both ships were destroyed. After *Sydney II* failed to return to port, air and sea searches were conducted. Boats and rafts carrying survivors from *Kormoran* were recovered at sea, while others made landfall at Quobba Station, where we stayed for one night. It is recorded that 318 of the 399 personnel on *Kormoran* survived. There were no survivors from the 645-strong complement on *Sydney II*. It remains Australia's worst naval disaster.

The two wrecks were discovered in 2008. The discovery failed to put to rest the ongoing controversy as to how and why a purpose-built warship such as *Sydney II* was defeated by a modified merchant vessel such as *Kormoran*. There have been numerous books written on the subject, as well as two official government inquiries in 1999 and 2009. According to German accounts *Sydney II* approached so close to *Kormoran* that the Australian cruiser lost the advantages of its heavier armour and superior gun range. But conspiracy theories abound.

The main memorial to *Sydney II* is in Geraldton. It is remarkable. The memorial includes 5 major elements: a stele of the same size and shape of the ship's prow (I felt so small next to it), a granite wall listing the ship's company, a bronze statue of a woman looking out to sea and waiting in vain for the warship to come home, the 'dome of souls' containing 645 welded stainless steel seagulls, and the pool of remembrance containing a map of the region and the marked position of *Sydney II*'s wreck. It all adds to a sorrowful experience when you walk slowly through each part. More than ever, I value living in peaceful times.

CHAPTER 24

How fearless were they?

WHEN EUROPEANS STARTED TO ARRIVE in Australia, there was a big country to explore. It was done by sea at first and then on land. We followed the routes of some of the most incredible journeys you could ever imagine. We did it in our comfortable motorhome with food and water always available. We pondered the true grit and resilience of the early explorers as they crisscrossed this vast dry land on horses, in small boats or on foot. They were totally fearless. Yet, the Aboriginal people did the same for thousands of years. It is important to acknowledge the significant contribution to the opening of Australia by Aboriginal people who assisted many of the early settlers and explorers. They helped them to find the food and the water required to continue onward. So please, take with a grain of salt the 'discoveries' made by the following explorers as they certainly did not find anything new. They just gave them different names. Still, their exploits are to be commended.

John Oxley

You cannot go anywhere in the interior of New South Wales without seeing John Oxley's name or a statue dedicated to him. Oxley was born in 1784 in Yorkshire and joined the Royal Navy at age 15 where he worked until 1811. He then moved to Sydney to take up a position as Surveyor-General. In that role, he was instructed by Governor Lachlan Macquarie to go find fertile land. Oxley led two expeditions during which he discovered two main rivers he named conveniently Lachlan and Macquarie Rivers. He wanted to find the source of the rivers, but try as hard as he could, he was always stopped by unpassable swamps. This led him to believe that the rivers ended in an interior sea. Thus began the myth of the Australian inland sea that other travellers bought into. But there had not been such a sea in central Australia for many thousands of years, as was proven by the explorers who came after him.

The towns of Dubbo, Tamworth and Forbes all owe their existence to Oxley. He crossed the Great Dividing Range to find the fertile plains he was looking for. He also went north and explored Southeast Queensland. He picked the spot for a special colony for difficult convicts in Moreton Bay, near where Chris and I live. He named the Brisbane River. There are suburbs, parks and streets named after him to commemorate his endeavours. His expeditions were so arduous that he suffered with illness throughout his service. He died on his property in New South Wales, aged 44.

Charles Sturt

Charles Stuart was born in 1795 in British India to poor parents. His father strongly advised his son to join the British Army since they could not pay for higher education. After postings in Canada, in 1827 Sturt found himself on the crew to accompany a ship of convicts to Sydney. He decided after landing here that Australia would become his home. Governor Darling of New South Wales instructed Sturt to explore the Australian continent. He became acquainted with John Oxley and wanted to follow in his footsteps in the discovery of the rivers. He started with the Macquarie, Bogan and Castlereagh rivers. He also came across the Darling River and unfortunately did not realise its importance.

His expedition of 1828–29 proved that northern New South Wales was not an inland sea. But still nobody knew where the western-flowing rivers of New South Wales went, so another expedition was approved by the governor. In January 1830, Charles Sturt and his party began their eventful voyage down the Murrumbidgee River. They soon reached the confluence with a much larger river, the Murray River, named by Sturt. They continued their journey down the Murray, east to west.

They confirmed that all the western-flowing rivers eventually flow into the Murray. One month later, they reached a large lake they called Lake Alexandrina. And in just a few more days they saw the deep blue sea of the Southern Ocean where they were disappointed. The mouth of the Murray was not suitable for shipping. I went searching for it myself and found it near Goolwa. It was the most dissatisfying thing I had ever seen. The smallest mouth surrounded by lagoons and sandbars. I could totally empathise with them.

But my search did not affect me like it did Captain Sturt. He went blind for several months and never fully restored his health. By the time they reached Sydney again, they had rowed and sailed nearly 2,900 kilometres of the river system–another feat of unbelievable endurance. Sturt's expedition led to the colony of South Australia being established.

Sturt was not finished with exploring and he still had a personal goal to achieve: to be the first white man to leave his footprint in 'the centre' of Australia. In August 1844, he set out to do just that. He put an expedition party together and travelled again along the Murray and Darling rivers. When they came to what would become Broken Hill, the extreme heat of the dry season put a stop to their progress for months. Eventually, the wet season kicked in and they continued forward. It was not in any way easier as they entered the deserts. They are known now as Sturt's Stony Desert and Simpson Desert. They could only go so far and had to turn around eventually. Sturt was not an easily deterred man and he went back a second time. He got scurvy, became very ill and had to give up his dream. Dr John Harris Browne, the expedition surgeon, became the leader of the party. After travelling a total of 4,800 kilometres, the whole expedition crew survived the trek.

Charles Sturt died at the age of 74. He has a national park, a highway, a university, a river, a desert and two flowers named after him.

Edward John Eyre

Edward John Eyre was an interesting character. I grew to both admire him and loathe him. Eyre was born in England in 1815. He moved to Sydney as a 17-year-old rather than join the army or go to university. Eyre soon displayed his flair for self-reliant leadership and adventure, buying 400 lambs one month before his 18th birthday. He became one of the early drovers in 1837 between New South Wales and South Australia and sold his livestock for a large profit. With the money from the sale, he set out to explore the interior of South Australia. He went on three expeditions to the Flinders Ranges and the surrounding deserts before his most memorable adventure.

Eyre, together with his 17-year-old Aboriginal companion Wylie, was the first European to traverse the coastline of the Great Australian Bight and the Nullarbor Plain by land in 1840–41, on a 3,200-kilometre trip to Albany, Western Australia. It was a journey of hardship, heat, exhaustion, hunger and thirst. He had originally led the expedition with John Baxter and three Aboriginal men. On 29 April 1841, two Aboriginals killed Baxter and left with most of their supplies. Eyre and Wylie survived only because they encountered a French whaling ship near Esperance (WA). After a fortnight spent recuperating aboard, the two persevered through torrential rain, swamps and freezing nights, arriving in Albany on 7 July 1841. Eyre returned to England in 1845 and published a chronicle of his travels. For his efforts Eyre was awarded the Royal Geographical Society's medal in 1847.

It is at this point that Eyre's life story takes an unexpected turn. He plunged into political appointments as Lieutenant Governor of New Zealand (1846–53) and of St Vincent in the West

Indies (1854–60). He was promoted to Acting Governor of two other colonies to finish as Governor of Jamaica. On 11 October 1865, the native inhabitants began to rebel at Morant Bay. This was quickly squashed and more than 400 were executed by Eyre's order. To make things worse, a few months later, he abolished the island's legislature and the Jamaican constitution. Jamaica became a crown colony.

The British intellectual elite were incensed by Eyre's behaviour and supported his trial for murder. But a grand jury in London declined to indict him for murder. A Royal Commission found Eyre innocent but condemned his 'unnecessary rigour'.

He died in 1901. He has a lake, a peninsula, a creek, a highway, streets, and villages named after him. My favourite memorial is the rusty iron sculpture of Eyre and Wylie at the lookout in Kimba, South Australia.

John Forrest

Sir John Forrest was born on August 22, 1847, near Bunbury in Western Australia. His achievements are well documented throughout that state. We were unaware of this gentleman until we came across many of his memorials.

Forrest was a surveyor in 1869 when he led a party through an unknown region near modern-day Laverton. The next year, he decided to retrace Eyre's journey through the Nullarbor but in the opposite direction, from west to east. Remember, Eyre's journey 30 years earlier had been a disaster that he endured for 12 months. On the other hand, Forrest was meticulous in his preparation and successfully completed the journey in 5 months. Moreover, nobody suffered ill health.

In 1874, Forrest journeyed from Geraldton (WA) to South Australia: 4,300 kilometres through very arid terrain. That was a tough gig. He became a well-sought-after public speaker in London the next year. He wrote two books about his three trips.

To me, the most noteworthy fact of all is that in all his exploration journeys, John Forrest had one constant companion, Tommy Windich. He was an Aboriginal man of the Kokar people famous for his tracking, horse riding, marksmanship skills and knowledge. When Tommy died in 1876, John Forrest had the most heart-warming farewell for Tommy. He said 'his name is almost a household word in this colony.... I feel that I have lost an old and well-tried companion and friend'.

In 1918, John Forrest became the first person born in Australia to enter the British peerage. He died not long after on board the troopship *Marathon* while on his way to London for medical treatment.

There is a national park, a river, many suburbs, and a hotel in Bunbury Western Australia named after him.

Burke and Wills

These two men–Burke and Wills–are forever linked and need no introduction to the average Australian. They are Robert O'Hara

Burke and William John Wills who, on the 20th of August 1860, left Melbourne (VIC) with the hope to be the first white people to cross the continent from south to north. The party consisted of 19 men of different nationalities. They took 23 horses, 6 wagons and 26 camels. They had three goals: scientific discovery, seeking new grazing land and finding a route for an overland telegraph line. The expedition was funded by the Victorian Government and the Royal Society of Victoria, who wanted to maintain Victoria's position as the 'most advanced' colony. Four of the party–Burke, Wills, Gray and King– did reach the Gulf of Carpentaria on the 9th of February 1861.

It became the most expensive expedition in Australian history. The leader Robert O'Hara Burke, an Irishman, had no exploration experience or skills in surveying or navigation. One wonders how he got the job. The inventory included 50 gallons of rum to 'revive tired camels' and an oak table. What could go wrong?

Twice Burke divided the party into smaller advance parties, creating depots along the way to restock with on the return journey. Burke, Wills, Gray and King departed Cooper Creek as their final depot. William Brahe was left in charge with instructions to wait three months for their return. To his credit, he waited four months before turning back on 21st of April 1861. Brahe buried a cache of food and a note stating his intention at the foot of a coolabah tree. Into the tree he engraved the directions, 'DIG 3FT NW APR 21, 1861'. The tree has entered Australian folklore as the 'Dig Tree' (we saw it and took time to reflect because the rest of the story saddened us).

In the meantime, Gray had died from malnutrition. And only *9 hours* after Brahe departed, Burke, Wills and King arrived at the Dig Tree. Fortunately, they found the cache with enough supplies to last them a month. They buried a message of their own under the Dig Tree explaining their plans. They decided to not retrace their steps to Menindee where the other depot was. Instead, they went southwest to reach a station at Mount Hopeless. That name alone should have been a sign not to go there. They never made it.

Search parties were sent and through a series of miscommunications–that second letter at the Dig Tree was never found–they kept missing each other. At the end of June 1861, Wills died alone, having urged the other two to leave him and keep searching for the Yandruwandha people who had been generous with their food and hospitality since the expeditioners had arrived at Cooper Creek. Then a few days later Burke died. King eventually found the Yandruwandha people who saved his life. Burke and Wills both died of malnutrition. Their bodies were found and buried. They were given Australia's first state funeral on 21 January 1863.

We found their last camp numbered B/CXIX (119). It is a heritage-listed site now on a private road near Normanton (QLD). Unusually, it was well signed and easy to locate. The expedition party had blazed 15 trees to mark its location. We walked around the 10 trees left, each with a small plaque. Tree Number 9 is believed to have vanished in 1997 and Number 1 was destroyed in 1999. Tree Number 6 was removed to be housed in a steel cage near the Normanton Railway Museum where we saw it. Why would they move that tree there?

While Burke, Wills, King and Gray were the first Europeans to cross Australia from south to north, it was Charles Sturt who found an all-weather route from Adelaide to the Arafura Sea in 1862.

There are many monuments and sculptures dedicated to the two iconic explorers. Several films and documentaries have been made about the crossing of Australia through the middle, including one narrated by David Attenborough in 1975.

We are in awe of the drive and fearlessness of those early explorers who, with sheer guts and determination, opened up this continent for the rest of us. I will never complain about a bad dirt road again.

CHAPTER 25

Who invented that?

THEY SAY THAT NECESSITY IS the mother of invention. Australia must have had a lot of necessity because many famous inventions were created here. The list is extraordinary, from Granny Smith apples to the Black Box Flight recorder and everything in between. Some people see a problem and will not rest until it is resolved. We all benefit now from their ingenious dedication even though we may not realise it.

Stump jump plough

I had heard about this invention, the stump jump plough, but I never took a serious interest in it as it was just 'farming stuff' to me. But it all became clear how important this item was when we visited Ardrossan (SA). That is where in 1876, two brothers developed a plough that could jump over stumps and stones, enabling newly cleared land to be cultivated. The problem they fixed was the mallee scrub issue, where the trees were impossible to remove. They would regrow after fire, being cut down or other kinds of damage. Their unbelievably large roots remained in the ground, making it difficult to plough the soil. The South Australian government offered a substantial reward for the invention of an effective machine that would remove the stumps.

That is when an agricultural machinery apprentice named Richard Bowyer Smith invented the device that revolutionised the industry. He accidentally discovered the principle of the stump jump plough when he used a plough that had some bolts missing. It was later developed and perfected by his brother Clarence Herbert Smith. The plough consisted of three hinged pivoting blades that worked independently of each other. When the blade encountered an underground obstacle like a mallee stump, it would rise out of the ground. Attached weights forced the blade back into the ground after the root was passed, allowing as much of the ground to be furrowed as possible. It did not remove the stumps but found a way to work around them. It was given the logical name, Stump Jump Plough. It was later regarded as one of the most important agricultural inventions of the century. It was eventually used throughout the British Commonwealth, transforming agricultural practices wherever it was adopted.

The brothers' factory, which grew to a great size, is partly preserved in Ardrossan and is now a museum. There is a stump jump plough on display indoors and another one outdoors on top of the cliff in town.

Feature film

I love movies and going to the cinema. It is a little known fact that the world's first full-length narrative feature film was *The story of the Kelly Gang*, filmed in Australia in 1906. The one-hour-long bushranger film traced the exploits of the nineteenth-century bushranger and outlaw Ned Kelly and his gang (see next chapter). It was shot in and around the city of Melbourne (VIC) and became a commercial and critical success. However, it was not without controversy. Some politicians and the police understood the film as a glorification of crime. The film was banned in certain parts of the country. Nevertheless, the film toured Australia for over 20 years and was also shown in New Zealand, Ireland and Britain.

Since its release, a dozen other films have been made about the Kelly legend. The most remarkable one is from 1970 and features Mick Jagger who plays Ned Kelly. Who would have thought that was a role for a rock and roller?

We learned more about Ned Kelly and his gang of misfits when we visited Beechworth in Victoria. The town and the surrounding bushland are linked to the life and times of the infamous Ned Kelly. We toured the historic courthouse where Ned was committed for trial, which sealed his fate in 1880. I took the judge's seat and Chris sat where Ned Kelly sat. I even used the gavel to bring the court to order. The guided tour was a real eye opener. There are two sides to each story. Ned and his family faced incredible hardships. There is more on that in the next chapter.

Stobie pole

I started seeing some unusual power poles in the south of Western Australia. Chris knew right away what they were–Stobie poles. They were invented in 1924 by an Adelaide Electric Supply Company engineer named James Cyril Stobie. Unlike the timber poles, they are made of two steel joists held apart by a slab of concrete. They are virtually indestructible. The problem they solved was the shortage of suitably long strong, straight and termite-resistant timber in South Australia. They were relatively cheap and simple to produce, had a uniform appearance, saved an enormous amount of timber from being harvested, had a long-life expectancy and, at the time, were seen as eco-friendly. They resist bushfire and flooding events. On the minus side, they are more susceptible to lightning strikes.

Stobies have continued to be used all over Australia. Each year South Australia Power Networks manufactures around 4,500 Stobie poles.

Since the 1980s, many Stobie poles have been decorated with artworks or surrounded with plants to beautify them. Artists have to request permission from the electricity/energy company first. Let's be honest, Stobie poles are ugly! Any effort to enhance their appearance should be welcomed with open arms.

Wine cask

It was certainly a novelty the first time I saw a wine cask in Australia. I had never seen nor tasted wine in a bag in Canada. It is only recently that I discovered that the cask was developed here in 1965. Once again South Australia was the birthplace of another invention that is now used worldwide. The humble wine cask was invented by Thomas Angove in Renmark (SA). Bulk wine used to be available in 2.25 litre flagons. The problem was that once the flagon was opened, the wine wouldn't keep for long. This led either to a waste of wine or excessive consumption. Tom Angove found the solution.

For those of you who only drink wine out of a bottle, the wine cask is a cardboard box housing a soft plastic bag, which collapses inside the carton as the wine is drawn off, thus preventing contact with the air. Angove's original design with a resealable spout was replaced with a tap by the Penfolds wine company in 1972.

The poor wine cask suffered derision for many years and had a bad reputation. It was thought to only contain poor quality wine for easy resale. But it is gaining more and more respect. Many wineries now pour the same wine into casks and bottles. It may be hard to believe, but there is even an international wine-in-a-box competition in *France*, awarding prizes for the best boxed wines. Cask wine has come a long way from its humble beginnings.

The facts speak for themselves. There are genuine benefits to drinking wine from a box:

1. Freshness: oxygen cannot get in and ruin the wine
2. Value: one 4 litre cask equals 5 bottles at a much cheaper price
3. Less packaging
4. Convenience: easy to open and serve just one glass if that is all you want
5. Rugged and portable: won't break in transit unlike glass bottles

Australians have several funny names for cask wine like my favourite, 'Chateau Cardboard'. It is also referred to as the 'Dubbo Handbag' (with variants of the same depending on location) or 'vino collapso'. I love the Aussie sense of humour!

CHAPTER 26

Is that a gun in your pocket?

BUSHRANGERS ARE POPULAR IN AUSTRALIA. I was never taken in by the general admiration of those criminals who robbed and killed people including police officers. I suppose I did not understand that they represented the secret desire by many people to just tell the authorities to go to hell. It is still a part of the Australian attitude, maybe dating back to the poor convicts brought here against their will.

Bushrangers may have been the first typically Australian characters to gain international recognition. They say that 'bad publicity is good publicity'. Some bushrangers achieved the status of folk heroes and were admired for their colourful personalities. They entered popular culture with a certain aura of romanticism. But all is not what it appears. Bushrangers led lives that were far from glamourous, often of a nasty nature and short duration.

Bushrangers were escaped convicts in the early years of the British colony. The bush was their protection from the police who were constantly on their tails. In 1805, a column in a Sydney newspaper mentioned the term 'bushranger' and it became part of the vernacular after that. The wealth created with the gold rush years from the 1850s to 1860s gave birth to a rise in crime. Typically, bushrangers robbed small-town banks and coach services. Eventually, bushranging as a career died off due to better policing and improvements in telecommunications. It is believed that over 2,000 bushrangers roamed the Australian countryside. There are countless songs, books, films, television series and sculptures dedicated to the bushranging folklore.

We came across some fascinating bushranger characters along the way. Here are the most noteworthy.

Ben Hall

We seemed to follow in Ben Hall's footsteps for a while in Central New South Wales. He was born in Maitland in 1837. His parents had been sent to the colony as convicts. Ben Hall and his gang of bandits carried out many raids from Bathurst to Forbes. To his credit, Hall was not directly responsible for any deaths, although several of his associates were.

From 1863 to 1865, over 100 robberies were attributed to Ben Hall and his gang, making them some of the most prolific bushrangers in that period. They held up several towns and dozens of mail coaches, and even stole prized racehorses.

On 5 May 1865, at dawn, Hall was ambushed by 8 policemen who shot him at least 30 times as he was trying to run away. The police claimed that they were acting under the protection of the Felons Apprehension Act 1865, which allowed any bushranger named under the terms of the Act to be shot and killed without warning by anyone. At that time, however, the Act had not yet come into force. So, the legality of Hall's killing was controversial.

We went looking for his grave and heritage-listed headstone in the Forbes cemetery. It was well signed, and we found it easily. He was only 27 when he died.

Hall is a prominent figure in Australian folklore, inspiring many bush ballads, books and screen works, including a 2016 feature film. We thought it was fitting to watch the movie *The Legend of Ben Hall* on YouTube the night we stayed in Forbes. It is not a great movie but it was informative.

Ned Kelly

Ned Kelly needs no introduction as he is the most well-known bushranger in Australia's history. He was born in 1855 to an Irish family that was often in trouble with the police. The apple does not fall far from the tree and Ned got himself into conflict early in life. At only 14, he was arrested for stealing money from a Chinese man. He spent 10 days in the police lockup but was set free due to insufficient proof. He was in and out of jail after that many times.

After fighting a policeman at his home in 1878, Kelly went to the bush to hide. He murdered three policemen who were searching for him. The government made Ned, his brother and two friends outlaws. They became known as the Kelly Gang. Ned Kelly led the gang to rob a number of banks, and even held up an entire town. The government had had enough and resorted to extreme measures to capture them.

A final violent battle with 46 policemen took place at the Glenrowan Hotel in 1880. Kelly and his acolytes, dressed in heavy homemade metal armour and helmets, were ready to fight to the bitter end. It is estimated that 15,000 bullets were fired during the battle. The police had even ordered a cannon from Melbourne, but it had not arrived. They set fire to the building instead. The shooting went on all night.

At dawn on the 28th of June, Ned Kelly came out of the hotel wearing his legendary armour. He marched towards the police, firing his gun at them. Their bullets bounced off his armour. Ned was shot in his legs, which were not protected by the armour. His brother Dan and Steve Hart may have killed themselves as their bodies were found lying side by side in a back room. They had taken off their armour. Joe Byrne died in the front room of the hotel from blood loss after a gunshot cut his femoral artery.

Several hostages were shot and three died, including 13-year-old Jack Jones, the son of the hotel owner.

Ned was taken to the Melbourne Gaol where he was treated for his wounds. He was visited by his mother who was in the same prison for wounding a police officer–a feisty family to be sure. In August, he was taken back to Beechworth by train for the first court hearings. This is the court we visited as mentioned in the previous chapter. Because the authorities feared a sympathetic local jury the trial was moved to Melbourne where they hoped the populace would not regard him as such a hero. Ned Kelly was found guilty of two murders. He was sentenced to death. Many people did not agree with the death sentence. A petition with more than 60,000 names asked the government for mercy. This gives you some idea of the extent of Ned's popularity. It was to no avail, and he was hanged on 11th of November 1880 at the tender age of 25.

Ned Kelly is still a major part of Australian popular culture. His story has been told in books, movies, plays and television shows. In 2010, the National Gallery of Victoria paid AU$2.2 million for a painting of Ned Kelly by artist Sidney Nolan. He even featured in the opening ceremony of the 2000 Summer Olympics in Sydney.

Captain Thunderbolt

There is a picturesque country road in New South Wales called Thunderbolt's Way. It weaves its way along 305 kilometres from coastal hinterland to mountainous high country. We thought it was one of Australia's most beautiful drives. Construction of the road began in 1958 and was completed three years later. We did the section between Gloucester and Uralla, about 200 kilometres. It gave us the opportunity to learn more about Australia's 'gentleman bushranger Fred Ward', alias Captain Thunderbolt. He roamed these parts in the early 1800s.

Frederick Wordsworth Ward was born in 1835, the son of a convict and the youngest of 10 children. He was renowned for escaping from Cockatoo Island and for being the longest-roaming bushranger in Australian history. Over 6-and-a-half years, Ward robbed mailmen, travellers, inns, stores and stations across much of northern New South Wales, from the Hunter Region north to Queensland. There is no evidence Fred Ward actually ever shot at anyone during his bushranging career. He would show his guns rather than discharge them, relying on his superior horsemanship for a quick getaway.

On 25 May 1870, 'Captain Thunderbolt' was shot and killed by Constable Walker near Uralla after allegedly robbing travellers. Apparently, Ward had been drinking in the local pub and may have had one too many drinks. Publican John Blanch served the outlaw's last drinks at gun point. Some people really want that last drink, and it was Ward's last!

There is a life-size statue of Captain Thunderbolt designed and cast by sculptor, Denis Adams. It was unveiled with much pomp and ceremony in 1988 in Uralla. It is easily visible on the highway going through town.

John Francis Peggotty

I have kept the best one for last. This bushranger is unknown to most people. He is far from being famous anywhere but in his home state of South Australia. John Francis Peggotty, known as the 'Birdman of the Coorong', was unique in pursuing his profession on the back of an ostrich! We discovered his legend by pure chance when we had a pit stop in Meningie and saw a weird statue in the park on the foreshore. The council erected a sculpture of an ostrich wearing a riding saddle in commemoration of Peggotty in 2013.

John Francis Peggotty was born in 1864 in Ireland. They say he rode an ostrich and wore large amounts of gold jewellery while committing his crimes. He preferred to wear his wealth. He was a small man due to being born three months premature.

As a young man, Peggotty travelled to South Africa where he learned how to ride ostriches. He then came back to England where he began breaking into houses by climbing down the chimneys. He was caught and served a 5-year prison sentence in England, after which he emigrated to Australia. He promptly resumed his criminal activity in Adelaide. He moved to the Coorong region in 1898 and became a bushranger. Riding on his ostrich, Peggotty would surprise his victims with his appearance, holding them up with a pair of small pistols. Peggotty was always too fast to catch and he escaped the police countless times. He is believed to have committed at least 12 hold-ups.

On the 17th of September 1899, Peggotty and his ostrich were shot and wounded by a man he was holding up near Meningie. Peggotty fled on the wounded animal. While the ostrich's body was recovered, Peggotty was never seen again.

Well, there are no records and no news articles to corroborate any part of that story. You might have already guessed that it is all made up. Meningie needed to attract tourists after a long period of drought. So, in 2013 this devious plan was concocted to test the gullibility of unsuspecting travellers. We fell for it hook, line and sinker. The life-size climbable statue is not even an ostrich, but an emu painted to look like an ostrich!

CHAPTER 27

Where did they come from?

WE KNOW THE FIRST NATIONS originated from Africa, as we all did. But after them, this country was founded on immigration from the moment the penal colony was settled in Botany Bay in 1788. Later on, when all the riches of the land were discovered, people came en masse to partake in the spoils. On our trip, we read incredible migration tales that are worth recounting.

The Chinese

Robe is a small coastal town in South Australia, which we visited on a rainy day. Little did we know what we would find there. A timber arch with a red sign on top standing in the shallow water caught my attention. Then I saw an unassuming rock memorial standing on the foreshore–a bronze plaque with writings in Chinese characters and English. The monument was erected in 1986 and consists of a 3-metre-high stone with pictures of a ship, a spade, a pick, a gold pan and Chinese people carrying their belongings on poles. *So, the Chinese were here, but why?* I was intrigued.

I learned that Robe was a small, isolated community of about 200 people when it became the starting point for a significant trek in Australian history. Thousands of Chinese left China and landed in the local bay after a long and difficult sea journey. They then walked overland through the bush for around 400 kilometres to reach the Victorian goldfields.

The number of Chinese prospectors ballooned so much that in 1855 the Victorian government taxed every immigrant £10 each. A cheaper port had to be found. Robe in South Australia was near the Victorian border and the welcoming South Australian government charged a landing fee of one pound: it was a no-brainer.

Chinese miners arrived in Robe in 1856, travelling by coastal steamer from Port Adelaide and Sydney. Then in 1857, they began arriving directly from overseas, 15,000 landing in that year alone. This must have been an incredible sight, just as it would be today. A total of 32 ships brought thousands of Chinese men and one woman.

In Robe harbour, cargoes of opium and tea were exchanged for wood, which was shipped to Melbourne. Residents also engaged in salvage operations when three of the ships carrying Chinese passengers were wrecked. The Chinese ships brought great prosperity to Robe, and most of the historic buildings were erected in this period.

But this was not the only gold rush to bring migrants from faraway places.

The Afghans

In the late 1890s, the gold rush in the deserts of Western Australia was on. Horses struggled due to the soft sand and intense heat. Camels were ideal to build train lines and roads, and to traverse the harsh deserts. The first camel called Harry (can you believe that name?) arrived in 1840. But two years before, in 1938, the first cameleers–camel drivers–arrived in South Australia.

These Afghan cameleers came to help with exploring the interior of the country. They were called 'Afghans' but were not solely from Afghanistan. They also came from nearby countries such as Egypt, Iran, Turkey, India and Pakistan. They were masters at handling camels. The majority arrived in Australia alone, leaving their families behind, and worked on three-year contracts. Approximately 20,000 camels and 2,000 cameleers arrived in Australia in the nineteenth century.

Many Afghans sought business opportunities in the goldfields. Their camels carried food and supplies to surveying and construction teams in the outback. The cameleers contributed greatly to the development of goldfield towns in Western Australia. But it was not an easy life.

The cameleers were subjected to brutal discrimination based on their appearance and religion. They were depicted unfavourably by journalists, and the government increased restrictions on them. Many cameleers were refused naturalisation because of the *Immigration Restriction Act* (White Australia Policy) of 1901–1958. When returning to work after visiting family abroad, they had to sit a dictation test, which many failed. They were refused re-entry to Australia.

Afghan influence stretched from one end of the country to the other, criss-crossing inland Australia. They played an extraordinarily important–and largely unacknowledged–part in our history. We did see a few memorials dedicated to the hard-working Afghans. And we encountered some businesses bearing names identifying their owners as descendants of the cameleers. We also visited cemeteries that had special sections for each religion, including Islam.

As for the camels, there are more than one million feral camels roaming the outback these days. We have the largest herd of camels in the world, many of which are exported to Gulf countries to be raced. How ironic is that? We only saw the tamed ones in Broome (WA) getting ready for their tourist sunset walk along Cable Beach.

THE EDUCATIONAL JOURNEY

CHAPTER 28

War: What is it good for?

I AM A PACIFIST, AND I will never understand the need to go to war or to invade a country. I do not comprehend what war is for. Nevertheless, the sacrifice of young people's lives on the frontlines can neither be ignored nor forgotten. This chapter looks at the two human sides of war: the people who go overseas to fight the war and the people who stay behind.

The war memorials

Australia, for such a young country, has fought in many wars and has lost too many soldiers per capita. Those hard facts are remembered in nearly every country town. We saw countless memorials on crossroads and in parks. Most are public works, but a few were built privately by grieving families to remember their loved ones who died on the other side of the world.

Australian individuals, and the country as a whole, are passionate about remembering the fallen more than 100 years after the first major military engagement in 1914. We have spent a lot of time, effort, and money to remember our war dead. Monuments started appearing in 1915 before the war was over. There are now over 5,000 monuments, cenotaphs, obelisks, shrines, arches, statues, pillars, cairns, flagpoles, walls, parks, and museums throughout Australia. The war memorials have special significance as they often represent 'surrogate graves' for soldiers who were buried in overseas war cemeteries or could not be located.

Unique to Australia, 90 per cent of town memorials list all the names of those who served in that town in alphabetical order. This helps meet the needs of the communities still grieving their loss. The passage of time does not seem to ease the pain. We saw many fresh floral wreaths around Anzac Day Commemorations on the 25th of April.

A common thread through the memorials is the poem 'For the fallen', written by English scholar Laurence Binyon in 1914:

> *They shall not grow old, as we*
> *that are left to grow old:*
>
> *Age shall not weary them, nor*
> *the years condemn,*
>
> *At the going down of the sun*
> *and in the morning*
>
> *We will remember them.*

This is often complemented with the inscription 'Lest we forget' from Rudyard Kipling's poem, *'Recessional'*. One cannot help being moved by those words.

Some memorials are truly welcomed places of reflection. On our mad trip, I sometimes sat in silence and just breathed in the serenity. This memorial in Onslow (WA) at sunset was an unforgettable sight. I am forever grateful to those who have sacrificed their lives.

WAR: WHAT IS IT GOOD FOR?

Internment / prisoner of war camps

Soldiers being conscripted and going to war is hard enough for me to understand. On the other hand, it is incomprehensible that many hard-working Australian citizens were put in internment camps *here* just because they were born in another country. That harsh fact opened my eyes to a whole new reality of the war in Australia. As a migrant myself, it hit quite close to home. It came to my attention for the first time when we visited Loveday in South Australia. Such a nice name for such a tainted place.

Let us review what happened.

During World War I and World War II, Australia held both military prisoners of war (POWs) and internees who were declared 'enemy aliens' from countries at war with Australia. Most were civilian men, but there were women and children as well. They were kept in camps, often in remote locations. People were interned based solely on their nationality, even if they had done no wrong.

In the First World War, about 7,000 people were imprisoned. Most of the internees were Germans. The camps were established

THE EDUCATIONAL JOURNEY

at Holsworthy, Liverpool, Berrima, Trial Bay (NSW) and Torrens Island (SA). The terms 'prisoner' and 'internee' were often used interchangeably. But the two groups had different rights and were treated differently by Australian authorities. POWs could be forced to work but internees could not. Internees had to be paid for any work they undertook by choice.

Australia's treatment of POWs in the war has been broadly considered fair. But the civilian internment remains a contentious issue. It is easy to understand how resentful many internees and their families would have felt. Some were born and raised in Australia from immigrant families and had lived here all their lives. They were caught in the net. Imagine coming here for a better life and ending up in jail due to a war that has nothing to do with you personally. I am heartbroken just thinking about it.

In the Second World War, Australia held more than 12,000 people in internment camps. There were 28 camps across all states. We visited two of them: Loveday (for civilians) and Cowra (for military personnel).

Loveday was established in 1941 and became the largest civilian internment camp in Australia. At Loveday, many of the internees chose to work outside the camp. It provided regular physical activity and contact with the world away from the barbed wire. Nonetheless, life was mostly boredom and frustration at the system that had locked them away without even being charged with any crime, let alone convicted.

The internment camp was approximately 440 acres and contained four sections. Only one internee escaped through the perimeter fence and nine escaped from working parties outside the compound. There was also a tunnel dug by some Germans that was discovered before it was fully completed. Jimmy James, the famous black tracker, always found the escapees. The Loveday Internment Camps were closed in 1946.

Our visit to the old camp site was sobering. We looked out across nice fields. Only a few buildings and some foundations are still standing. More details are available at the Loveday Internment

Camp Display housed in the Barmera Visitor Information Centre. There is a touching hologram experience not to be missed.

Cowra in New South Wales was a very different experience for so many reasons. The Cowra Prisoner of War Camp was constructed in 1941 to house 2,000 Italian POWs. In 1943, over 1,000 Japanese POWs arrived. By the end of June 1944, the camp was overcrowded. On the 5th of August 1944, the Japanese prisoners staged a breakout. It was a blood bath during which over 300 escaped (all were recaptured), 231 Japanese and four Australians died. Eighteen buildings were burned to the ground. This was the first time that war was fought on home soil, and it was the largest revolt of its kind in Australia's history.

After the end of the war, the camp and its surrounds were sold to the New South Wales Department of Agriculture and a private owner for grazing and farming. Part of the site remains within a public reserve where a walking trail goes through the camp ruins with many information panels. The town is also the site of the only Japanese War Cemetery in Australia.

The POW site has a particular cultural and spiritual significance to Japan as it was the focus of the breakout and loss of life of Japanese prisoners. Unique reconciliation efforts between Australia and Japan are visible in town. Links formed between Cowra and Japan have been instrumental in creating the identity of the town in the post-war period. We walked along the picturesque path in the Cowra Peace Precinct that finishes at the stunning Japanese Garden and Cultural Centre.

The Cowra Japanese Gardens are breathtaking. We spent considerable time walking amongst the perfectly manicured lawns and pathways. How amazing that from war can grow such beautiful cooperation between former enemy nations.

CHAPTER 29

What were they thinking?

THERE IS NOTHING LIKE A beautiful mind. I am a sapiophile if truth be known. Fortunately, this country has seen many brilliant thinkers, and it still does. Not all were born here, but many migrated here and put their thinking caps on and worked to make Australia what it is today. They are amongst others, the poets, founders of the federation and architects.

The poets

I have been writing poems since I was 16 years old. There is something magical in playing with words and rhymes. I love it, even if my level is basic. My husband Chris also writes poetry and we have written so many poems between us and for each other since we met. It was not a surprise then that we loved learning about Australian writing icons such as Banjo Paterson and Henry Lawson.

Banjo Paterson

I already alluded to Banjo in Chapter 10 when we stopped in Winton. He is one of Australia's favourite writers and arguably the best of them all, for good reasons.

Andrew Barton Paterson was born in 1864 in country New South Wales. His love of the Australian bush started in his childhood. He was fond of horses from an early age. He was an accomplished sportsman later in life, but his passion was horsemanship.

Paterson was a well-educated man who became a solicitor in Sydney in 1886. Around that time, he submitted his poems to newspapers to be published. He used the pseudonym 'The Banjo', the name of his favourite horse. He practised law until 1900 then switched to journalism, covering the Boer War, and travelling on assignment to China and the Philippines. Another career change saw him join the army in the First World War and he served in France and Egypt. After the war, Paterson returned to journalism.

The lyrics of the famous 'Waltzing Matilda' bush ballad were written in Winton (QLD) by Paterson. Incredibly, in 1981, Slim Dusty's version of the song 'Waltzing Matilda' was the first song broadcast by astronauts to Earth from the space shuttle. But it is more than a cherished folk song. 'Waltzing Matilda' is regarded widely as Australia's unofficial national anthem.

The information centre in Winton is called the Waltzing Matilda Centre. It is the only museum in the world to be dedicated to a song. The centre reopened in 2015 after a fire burnt it down. The complex is exquisite, from its amazing architecture to its informative content.

Another place we passed through accidentally, and which introduced me to another poem by Banjo Paterson, is Ironbark. Well, it used to be called Ironbark until the name was changed to the boring 'Stuart Town' in 1879. The town holds an annual bearded man festival contest after the Patterson's poem 'The man from Ironbark'–a most amusing read. I bet that would be quite something to attend.

Banjo Paterson died of a heart attack in Sydney in 1941 at the age of 76.

Henry Lawson

Around the same time that Banjo Paterson was writing, another bush poet was rising in notoriety. They were friends and were engaged in a gentle rivalry of verse about the charms of bush life. However, their lives could not have been more different.

Henry Lawson was born in 1867 (only three years after Banjo) in a tent on the Grenfell goldfields in New South Wales. He was the first of four children. His father was a gold prospector, and the family lived a nomadic lifestyle. Lawson consequently only received three years of formal schooling. But his mother Louisa Lawson was a published writer, a feminist and a political activist. She was an inspiring figure throughout Lawson's life.

Lawson was a shy boy and was bullied at school. A serious ear infection cost him most of his hearing by the age of 14. He later stated that his deafness led to his creativity as a writer. He wrote regularly into the 1890s but struggled with alcoholism and mental illness. He was spending more and more time in his favourite bars around Sydney, and his marriage fell apart. After periods of destitution, he would land in jail and psychiatric institutions.

In 1893, someone funded Lawson to take a trip to Bourke (NSW) in the countryside. It turned out to be one of the most important journeys of his life. It was the source of many of his bush poems and short stories such as 'The loaded dog', mentioned in Chapter 18.

Lawson was distressed by what he saw in the drought-ravaged west of New South Wales during his travels. He was appalled by the poor men begging for scraps and living like animals. He travelled with a swag and noticed a whole different way of living from what he was used to in the city. By the time Lawson went back to Sydney, he was armed with memories and experiences both funny and dramatic that would fuel his writing for years.

Nevertheless, Lawson's personal and literary life went into a downward spiral. In December 1902 he attempted suicide. His wife Bertha finally asked for a divorce in 1903 on the grounds of his drunkenness and physical violence, on top of emotional and psychological abuse.

Henry Lawson became a frail, haunted and pathetic man well known on the streets of Sydney. He died in 1922 at the age of 55 following a cerebral haemorrhage. Despite his sad ending, his contribution to Australian culture was so well recognised that he became the first Australian writer to be granted a state funeral.

The founders of the federation of Australia

Australia was a late bloomer in terms of becoming a fully grown country on the First of January 1901. From 1788 when the first convict ship landed in Botany Bay, the land had been split into eventually six British colonies (later called states) all doing their own thing in terms of defence, taxes, and transport with different gauges on their rail tracks. They even had their respective parliaments and navies, but the final law-making power was in the motherland.

It all became very inefficient and by the 1880s the colonists were discussing the possibility of a national government. The bigger issues of trade, defence and immigration indicated a need for a federation. Some voices advocating for the federation were louder than others.

John Forrest

John Forrest was mentioned in Chapter 25 for his role as an explorer. But he was so much more than that, as we found out travelling around Western Australia. He obviously also had a great mind, which he put to good use.

After his three successful exploration trips, Forrest was appointed Surveyor-General in 1883. The job came with a seat in the Legislative and Executive Councils, which acted as advisory bodies to the governor. This was his entrance in the political field. By the time Western Australia was granted a constitution in 1890, he became the colony's first premier. He held that position for the next decade. And what a decade it was.

Shortly after Forrest became premier, gold was discovered in Coolgardie (1892) and Kalgoorlie (1893). This led him to instigate a series of public civil works with engineer C Y O'Connor (see Chapter 34), which turned Western Australia's destiny around. He sponsored harbour works, railroad development and the golden pipeline project to supply water to the goldfields. He also worked for women's suffrage and for expanding land settlement. This was all happening at the same time as the Australian federation was being conceived. Forrest was a busy man!

In state negotiations for federation between 1887 and 1901, he advocated for the interests of the smaller states, winning railroad and tariff benefits for Western Australia. He tried hard to get more concessions for his home state but eventually voted 'yes' in the federation referendum. After federation, Forrest resigned as Premier of Western Australia and entered federal politics. He was elected unopposed as the Member for Swan. He was quickly promoted to different ministerial positions including treasurer until his death in 1918.

Forrest's legacy to Western Australia is highly visible everywhere you go. His reputation as a statesman was somehow tarnished, however, by his controversial views on Indigenous people. Even though he had travelled extensively with his valued companion Willy during his exploration days, he was recorded as labelling Aboriginal people as inferior in intelligence, comparing them to children.

Henry Parkes

Someone who has left a huge heritage in the state of New South Wales is Henry Parkes. Often called the 'Father of Federation', Parkes was born in England in 1815. From humble beginnings he rose to the highest political echelons. His formal education was limited. He started working at a young age as a labourer to help support his family. He migrated with his wife and arrived in Sydney in 1839. Parkes became a labourer with the Customs Department. As a side interest, he started writing poetry–an amazing endeavour for someone so poorly educated. He was only 27 when he published his first book of verse, *Stolen Moments*. He was also becoming more politically aware, and joined the Anti-Transportation League, which opposed convicts coming to New South Wales.

In 1850, he started the *Empire* newspaper, which soon became the colony's voice of freedom and democracy. He ran it until 1858.

In the meantime, he was elected in 1854 and served almost without interruption as a representative and often as a minister or premier until 1894. He served five terms as Premier of New South Wales between 1872 and 1891 and was knighted in 1877.

Parkes delivered his famous Tenterfield Oration in 1889, the first of a series of meetings that led to the federation of the six states of Australia. He went on to present the same speech 15 times in different locations over the next nine months. Henry Parkes was a man of great ambition, accomplishment and vision. He boasted that he would federate the colonies in 12 months. He was dreaming big and despite his best efforts, he did not live to see federation come to be. He died aged 81 in 1896, five years before his vision for Australia was achieved.

The architect

We followed the trail of one amazing man in Western Australia, John Hawes. He was distinctive in combining two careers: architecture and priesthood. We found out that he lived the most astonishing life.

John Hawes

John Cyril Hawes was born in 1876 in England. He came from a comfortable middle-class family. He studied to become an architect and started practising in 1897. He designed houses and won competitions for his excellent work, going on to build his first church in 1899.

He then turned his mind towards religion. He was ordained a Church of England priest in 1903 and worked in missions in England and the Bahamas. There, he combined his faith with architecture and kept designing churches.

Hawes left the Bahamas for the United States in 1911. He appeared to have lost his religion and went on to lead a nomadic existence in Canada and the United States for several years, including working as a labourer and as a railway teamster. He then decided to convert to Catholicism and became a Catholic priest in 1915.

The Church sent Hawes to Geraldton (WA) where he worked as a priest, architect and builder. That is where we first heard of Monsignor Hawes. We visited the Cathedral of St Francis Xavier, which he designed and helped to build with his own hands. He took his vow of service seriously. It was finally opened in 1938 after 22 years of hard work. This is one magnificent building. His work around the area was prolific. His name is all over town and the surrounding region where he designed more than 15 buildings. We accidentally discovered The Monsignor Hawes Heritage Trail when we landed in Mullewa (WA) where he lived for a few years. It is an interesting track to follow with information panels explaining his significant impact there and overseas.

After supposedly retiring from the priesthood in 1939, Hawes wanted to live as a hermit in the Bahamas, but he continued to build churches there. He died in 1956 in Florida and at his request was buried in a cave beneath the hermitage on Cat Island in the Bahamas.

John Hawes definitely lived a full life, and he left behind many fine monuments to his talent.

CHAPTER 30

Is our history black and white?

TO MY GREAT SHAME, I admit that I never had a meaningful encounter with an Indigenous Australian in the 23 years that I lived in New South Wales. It is only when I took up a post with Queensland Health as an occupational therapist in 2010 that I finally got to meet and work with Aboriginal health professionals. I also assisted Indigenous clients with mental health issues. I am someone who does not judge a book by its cover, and I believe in equality. We are all human beings. Certainly, my trip to South Africa and my visit to the Cradle of Humanity Museum in 2011 only reinforced my belief that we all come from the same place in Africa. To me, there is no black and white. But for Australian First Nations, it is a different story with not much grey in it. Our trip showed us the bad, the ugly and the good of the black and white relationships.

The bad and the ugly

Travelling in the remote areas of Australia, we saw with our own eyes the disparity in wealth between black and white. We also noticed the devastating effects of alcohol on communities. In one town, the local pub was entirely boarded up except for one small window just big enough to pass through a case of beer, which could be purchased and taken away. No drinking inside or outside the pub was allowed (we have already mentioned the different state laws for the sale of alcohol). We saw inebriated people walking and screaming at each other across the streets in the middle of the day. We drove past dilapidated houses and front yards full of junk. I felt so sorry for this state of affairs, and I don't have the solution to this challenging situation. Politicians keep pouring money into projects that don't seem to work.

It is heartbreaking when one learns more details about what the white men did to the black population since arriving here over 200 years ago. We stopped in many museums and looked at endless artifacts.

First, there were over 400 devastating massacres and mass poisonings of Aboriginal people on the continent. Historians talk of colonial genocide. It is hard to comprehend, but through these actions the First Nations population went from over one million people to less than 100,000 by the early 1900s. Their population has recovered, and the latest census has nearly one million people identifying as Indigenous.

Butterabby Graves

We came across very moving memorials. The first site was discovered accidentally when we visited Mullewa (WA). We saw a sign to the Butterabby Graves, which we followed not knowing what it was about. Butterabby Graves has significant historic value as a place where the Nhanhagardi/Wilunyu people resisted the spread of pastoral land and suffered the consequences. The government wanted to deter such resistance. Five Aboriginal people were hanged and buried in Butterabby in 1865 after they had been found guilty of spearing to death Thomas Bott. This is all in the context of conflict over limited food and water resources.

The site is on a low hill and includes a path with three random rubble grave mounds, a large granite memorial stone and a shelter shed with an eery laser cut steel roof with Aboriginal faces on it looking down at the visitors. Once seen it can never be forgotten. Their names were Wangayakoo, Yourmacarra, Garder, Charlacarra and Williacarra. When they were hanged the local Indigenous people were rounded up and made to watch the hanging of their people, presumably as a 'valuable lesson'. I cannot believe such cruelty towards fellow human beings.

Battle of Pinjarra Memorial Park

The second memorial we saw was a big rock with a plaque remembering the Battle of Pinjarra in Western Australia. The number of Binjareb people killed remains unknown but could be up to 30. The text on the plaque remembers those who died in 1834 without referring to a massacre as such: it is called a battle. There are now plans to rectify the situation and be more respectful of what really happened there. Since 1991, the *massacre* is annually remembered at that site by the Binjareb people on 28th of October.

There were more facts we picked up along the way such as the enslavement of free people to carry out hard labour, often in chains including a neck chain. There was the promotion of someone to be 'king' over other people with a breast plate to identify them: a concept alien to Aboriginal people. There was the *stolen generation* with its long-lasting impact and traumatic effect.

My heart aches for all the atrocities committed in the name of 'civilisation'. I am truly sorry they had to endure such inhumane treatment.

THE EDUCATIONAL JOURNEY

The good

On the other hand, there have been steps made towards reconciliation. For example, there was recognition on some historical plaques of the contribution of Indigenous people during settlement and during the war.

The Three Encounter Poles, Victor Harbor

I commend the council of Victor Harbor in South Australia in particular for their solid effort to right the wrongs of the past. As soon as you drive in the coastal town, you are face to face with a perplexing artwork on the Esplanade. It marks the 200th anniversary of Matthew Flinders' meeting with Nicholas Baudin in close-by Encounter Bay in 1802. Three vibrant 15-metre-high flag poles represent 'Three Worlds' and 'Three Cultures'. The poles recognise the association between the British, French, and Aboriginal cultures entwined through wind and water. It is very symbolic and poetic at the same time.

At the base in big letters is written 'On Occupied Territory'. It shocked me when I first read it and I did a double-take. What was it all about? It refers to the fact that in 1802 Australia was *occupied*. Matthew Flinders' charts refer to 'Terra Australis' and he acknowledged the local inhabitants as 'Australians' in his journal. This is contrary to what Captain James Cook did thirty years earlier when he claimed possession of the East Coast of Australia for Britain under the assumption of terra nullius. It was in accordance with the international law of Europe at the time. In 1835, New South Wales Governor Richard Bourke implemented the legal principle of terra nullius in Australian Law to justify British Settlement. This was famously overturned in the High Court of Australia in 1992 in the Mabo Case for Native Title in Queensland.

But Victor Harbor has gone even further than the artwork on the Esplanade. There is a genuine apology to the local Ngarrindjeri People written on a plaque:

> *To the Ngarrindjeri people, the traditional owners of the land and waters within the region. The City of Victor Harbor expresses sorrow and sincere regret for the suffering and injustice that you have experienced since colonisation and we share with you our feelings of shame and sorrow at the mistreatment your people have suffered.*
>
> *We respect your autonomy and uniqueness of your culture. We offer our support and commitment to your determination to empower your communities in the struggle for justice, freedom and protection of your Heritage, Culture and interests within the Council area and acknowledge your right to determine your future.*

We commit to work with you. We acknowledge your wisdom and we commit to ensuring our actions and expressions best assist your work. We accept your frustrations at our past ways of misunderstanding you.

We are shamed to acknowledge that there is still racism within our communities. We accept that our words must match our actions and we pledge to you that we will work to remove racism and ignorance.

We will recognise your leadership, we honour your visions, and we hope for a future of working together with respect for each other.

We look forward to achieving reconciliation with justice.

We walk beside you and stand with you to remedy the legacy of 166 years European occupation of your land and waters and control of your lives.

The work of the City of Victor Harbor will be guided by your vision of a future where reconciliation through agreement may be possible, and we may walk together.

The City of Victor Harbor acknowledges the Ngarrindjeri People's connection to the land and waters within its area and further acknowledges the Ngarrindjeri People's continued culture and interests therein.

Positive signs, Beagle Bay

Some Aboriginal communities like in Beagle Bay (WA), have taken unique steps to improve their situation. Beagle Bay is a medium-sized Aboriginal community on the western side of the Dampier Peninsula, north of Broome. There we saw signs everywhere with encouraging messages trying to steer young ones away from drugs and alcohol abuse.

We went there specifically to look at the Sacred Heart Church with its famous mother-of-pearl shell altar. This is one of the most beautiful churches I have ever seen and it is exceptional. The church was built entirely by hand by local Aboriginal people and the Pallottine monks who started the Catholic mission in the late 1800s. The area is home to the Nyul Nyul people who've existed in this harsh but pristine coastal environment for thousands of years.

Once used as a home for Aboriginal children separated from their families, it is now administered by those same children through the Billard Aboriginal Corporation. The monks are still there and are responsible for running the church and school.

We did not interact unfortunately with any native persons at Beagle Bay. The streets were deserted except for a few tourists at the church. But we did have four very pleasant experiences with Aboriginal people during our trip in other locations.

The first encounter was with an Indigenous Ranger in the Information Centre in Normanton (QLD). He was very friendly and engaged in a good chat. We were talking about crocodiles in the local river and how tourists ignored danger signs. He had met a few of them. But he also added that some of *his people* think they cannot get attacked because they are at one with nature. He called bullshit on that theory, and we all had a good laugh.

The second time we engaged with Aboriginal people was in Mark Norvall's Art Gallery in Derby (WA). It was so nice to walk out the back into the studio area and chat with the local artists at work. We were introduced to the Wandjina, a powerful rain maker spirit only seen in this part of Australia. Wandjina dreamtime images are painted in significant Aboriginal ritual sites, on rock galleries and in caves, throughout the region. The paintings, marked in red and white ochre, were traditionally repainted each decade to ensure the image was kept fresh and lively. I found them slightly scary to look at. They are very unusual.

Another wonderful encounter was in Carnarvon Information Centre (WA). The Indigenous art display was top class with beautiful pieces on the walls. The lady at reception told us she was also a painter who started late in life. She showed us her gorgeous dot paintings and real-life canvases. She also took the time to show us a few bits of bush tucker in the gardens. I can almost still taste the delightful, sweet nectar of native flowers we crushed with our hands.

But my best memory will be our conversation with two Aboriginal men while soaking in the hot spring bath in Walgett (NSW). It was rainy and there was nobody else but the four of us enjoying the warm water on a cold winter day. We started talking and they told us that it was emu eggs season. I asked how many eggs they took out of the nest. One man said he took all the eggs he could find. But the second man stated he always left two or three which is the accepted norm for sustainability. They both said they tasted delicious. Then, they told us about the Dark Emu and how it indicates that it is the right time to eat the eggs.

The night sky at that time of the year (May–June) reveals an emu near the Southern Cross constellation, which the Aboriginal people have known for thousands of years. I looked for that emu in the sky that night and the following nights but could not find it. I was starting to think they had fooled us with a fake folk story. But one week later during the telescope evening in Coonabarabran (NSW), the guide asked if we had heard of the dark emu in the sky.

Yes I said at once, 'and where is it?'

I was so excited when I finally spotted the huge emu's silhouette amongst the stars with the naked eye. It was true after all. The emu was a dark shape outlined by stars whereas I had been looking for an emu outline *made* of stars. That is why it is called the dark emu. Now you know too.

CHAPTER 31

Do you mine?

TRAVELLING THROUGH AUSTRALIA YOU SOON find out where the money is made and how it goes around. I used to read in the newspapers how Western Australia had a mining boom and lots of high paying jobs were begging for applicants. Now we understand just a little better the intricacies of the economy. It involves more than mines, but mines are a big part of it without a doubt.

We passed by at least 100 mineral mines. Most were operational, but many had closed down. The mind boggles at the amount of money that is made from extracting ore from our vast continent. You don't understand the magnitude of this industry until you see it with your own eyes.

There are more than 350 operating mines in this country. Australia is one of the world's leading producers of iron ore, lithium, gold, diamond and uranium. Moreover, we have large quantities of black coal, silver, copper and tin. Mining occurs in all states, but Western Australia is by far the leader of the pack. It is the resources export hub of Australia, producing more than 50 different minerals from about 125 sites.

Our two most important mineral commodities are iron ore and coal. The iron ore comes from 29 mines, 97 percent of which are located in Western Australia. And the coal comes from over 90 mines, mostly located in Queensland and New South Wales. Let us look closer at those two mammoth resources.

Iron

Iron is the fourth most common element in the Earth's crust. Australia is the largest exporter of iron ore in the world. It is a big business that requires trains to move the stuff around. We thought we had seen long coal trains in Queensland. We had seen nothing yet. The endless trains running 24 hours a day, just zigzagging in the dry landscape, were unforgettable. When stuck at a railway crossing and one of these monsters goes by in front of you, you feel quite small. They certainly command respect and patience as you wait a long time for them to pass.

The data is eye watering. Each train can have up to 270 cars. The average Pilbara (WA) iron ore train is two kilometres long and each load is worth roughly one million dollars. Some iron ore trains have made it into the Guinness Book of Records as the longest and heaviest trains in the world. The train that broke records was 7.3 kilometres long with 682 wagons. Amazingly, although the train had many locomotives, it was controlled by just one driver.

The most startling fact is that there are three mining companies each with their privately owned railway, up to 426 kilometres in length each. They are BHP (The Broken Hill Proprietary Company), Fortescue and Atlas Iron. They don't share their tracks and infrastructure. Therefore, there are three wharves and three fleets of tugboats in Port Hedland's harbour where everything is loaded onto ships destined for China. Within two weeks, the ships have unloaded and returned for the next load.

Port Hedland

Port Hedland's harbour is on a scale that cannot be appreciated until seen up close. It is a city that never sleeps. Move over New York! We did a tour run by the Port Hedland Seafarers Centre and a lap around the harbour in one of their Seafarers Launch Service boats. A guide provided a detailed and informative commentary and answered any questions, while two Ukrainian seafarers travelling with us were dropped back to their ship. It was fascinating to be involved for a few hours with this good Samaritan organisation.

Iron Knob

Good old Iron Knob in Western Australia (we are still chuckling at the name)! BHP started mining there in November 1899, the birthplace of iron ore mining in Australia. After nearly 100 years, mining at Iron Knob ended. The ore was of such high quality–nearly 60 percent pure–that BHP decided to create its own steel manufacturing plants in Newcastle and Port Kembla, in New South Wales.

The Community Tourist Centre in Iron Knob has been developed as a mining museum. It displays old mining equipment, mineral specimens, interpretive displays and photographs, and a theatrette that presents the story of mining in Iron Knob.

As we travelled, we saw enough giant trucks and other vehicles being transported from one mine site to another to constantly remind us of the iron ore industry. It runs this country.

Coal

The Queensland mining industry is the world's largest exporter of seaborne coal. We waited patiently *again* for many trains at crossings. Seventy trains travel daily along 2,670 kilometres of tracks. The Central Queensland Coal Network connects 50 mines with five major export ports on the east coast. We did not stop to visit the International Coal Centre open to the public in Blackwater, the coal capital of Australia. My reticence to patronise the fossil fuel industry stopped me from checking it out. It is ironic given we were driving a diesel guzzling bus around the countryside. I still feel guilty about that.

Gold

Australia is rich in gold and one of the world's top producers with about 60 percent found in Western Australia. The largest gold nugget ever discovered was the 'Welcome Stranger', found in 1869 at the base of a tree in Victoria. It weighed 70 kilograms and would be worth over $3 million today. WOW!

Mount Morgan

Our first gold mine sighting was in Mount Morgan (QLD) where a mine operated from 1882 until 1981. In 99 years, they extracted 225 tonnes of gold, 50 tonnes of silver and 360,000 tonnes of copper. You read that right. The mine was once the largest gold mine in the world even though it was primarily a copper mine. What a nice little bonus!

Now it is a big hole in the ground and a tourist attraction. The site contains the remaining structures of its mining operations including the General Office, Gold Rooms and Main Stack. There were no tours available, and we saw it all from the Arthur Timms lookout.

Apparently, the water in the pit contains elevated levels of copper, aluminium, magnesium, and other metals. This is a problem as during heavy rainfall the toxic water overflows into the local Dee River. Estimates for a partial rehabilitation of the toxic environmental legacy of the old gold mine start at $450 million. The company has long since been dissolved and nobody has put their hand up for that job yet.

Fimiston Open Pit, Kalgoorlie.

Gold, gold, and more gold was found in Kalgoorlie at the biggest thing we ever saw–Fimiston Open Pit known as the Super Pit. It is located in what was one of the richest gold deposits in the world, the Golden Mile, which was discovered during the 1893 gold rush. The Super Pit is about 3.5 kilometres long, 1.5 kilometres wide and 600 metres deep. It is big enough to be seen from space! It was the biggest open gold mine in Australia until 2016, when it was surpassed by the Boddington gold mine (WA). My mind struggles to imagine how large that pit is.

We could not resist the opportunity to view a working gold mine site and get right into the action with the big trucks all around us. So, we joined the mine bus tour. It took us through the high security gates past the mine site offices, Fimiston Mill, Workshop Yard (where they repair those massive trucks) and to an internal lookout. There we were able to get out of the bus and view the operation from a different perspective than the one at the Super Pit Lookout (we did go to that lookout afterward and spent time looking down at the massive hole). The tour was mesmerising and we got very good value for money. We were informed at the end that we all had gold dust *on and in us*. We were truly precious! We could see gold shimmering in the dust on the ground everywhere.

Montreal Goldfield

By contrast, the small, abandoned Montreal Goldfield was a totally different affair. It was Australia's only seaside goldfield in Bermagui (NSW). I simply had to visit this place with the name of my hometown. It was named by Henry Williams who was also from Montreal in Canada. In September 1880, gold was discovered *on the beach*. The rush lasted only three years, but nearly 250 kilograms of gold was unearthed using only picks and shovels. This goldfield is also home to the great unsolved Bermagui Mystery–the disappearance of a government surveyor and four miners. A lot of theories and conspiracies were revealed as part of the walking tour we took.

Watson was allowed to walk around with us and see the primitive shafts all dug by hand. There were signs everywhere to be careful and not fall in.

Perth Mint

After visiting gold mines, it was only logical to have a look at the Perth Mint where gold is processed and ready to market in different shapes, as gold bullion, coins or jewellery. We got to see the world's largest gold coin that weighs one tonne. It was cast in 2011 and travelled the world. It is now permanently secured in the Mint

THE EDUCATIONAL JOURNEY

where it was made. We witnessed a liquid gold pour in the original 1899 melting house. To see pure gold being heated to molten temperature and cooling down to form a solid gold bar right in front of our eyes was pretty amazing. 'All that glitters is not gold' does not apply in the Perth Mint.

We did learn how much our weight is worth in gold when we stepped on a special set of scales. I have kept the ticket to remind myself that I was once worth over $6 million! Not bad. I told my husband he could not afford me.

Salt

After all the precious metals, the other mines we saw were salt mines–so many! Western Australia is a major producer, accounting for around 80 percent of Australian production, followed by South Australia with minor amounts in Victoria and Queensland.

Common salt is one of the most widely used substances on the planet, with around 14,000 reported uses. The largest source is in the world's oceans. Therefore, most of the world's salt supplies are obtained by solar evaporation of seawater, which is the only renewable commodity in the world. As it happens, Australia is a big island surrounded by plenty of oceans. It is no surprise then that we make so much salt. It all makes sense now but take everything I say with a grain of salt.

Damper Salt Limited

Dampier Salt Limited (DSL) in Western Australia is the world's largest exporter of seaborne salt. We drove past its three solar salt operations in Dampier, Port Hedland and Lake MacLeod. Combined, they produce approximately 10.3 million tonnes of salt every year. Those blinding white mountains of crystals are a striking sight in the flat landscape. You never look at table salt the same way after seeing so much salt laying around.

DO YOU MINE?

CHAPTER 32

Are diamonds a girl's best friend?

I AM NOT A FAN of jewellery, and I wear only a few rings with sentimental value. Diamonds are not my best friends. But no one can deny the appeal of shiny objects. Precious gems fall into that category. Out of 4,000 different minerals, only 130 are considered gemstones. In addition, organic materials that are not minerals, such as amber or pearl, are also often considered to be precious.

The rarest and most valuable gems are diamond, emerald, sapphire and ruby. Australia opted for opal as its national gemstone. We encountered many opportunities to go fossicking for precious stones, but it is not our thing. Maybe we should have because someone in 2020 found a 424-carat sapphire in the gem fields of central Australia worth $300,000!

Diamonds

I have already mentioned our flight over Lake Argyle and the Ord River. It included flying over the open cut Argyle mine, now just a huge hole in the ground. The mine site covers about 124 acres: 1,600 metres long and down to 600 metres. It closed in November 2020. The Rio Tinto operation in Western Australia's remote Kimberley region had operated for 37 years. It produced around 95 percent of the world's supply of the famous pink diamonds. They also extracted other colours of diamonds: white, champagne, cognac, blue, violet and red. I did not know they came in so many colours. More than 865 million carats of rough diamonds were extracted from the red soil. It started by using open-pit techniques but that stopped in 2010. The operations went underground three years later. Unfortunately, the diamonds were generally of an average quality with only five percent of gem quality. Nevertheless, the mine was still viable and sustainable due to the high yield.

The company has now committed to respectfully rehabilitating the mine and returning the land to its traditional custodians. That's a good thing.

Opals

If I had to choose a favourite gem, it would be sapphire because blue is my favourite colour. But opals would come second due to their magnificent colourful appearance. Australia trades 95 percent of the world's supply. It is a little-known fact that opals are rarer than diamonds.

There are numerous opal mining towns in Australia where miners try to get rich. They are often wild and unruly places surrounded by a moonscape-like scenery with small hills everywhere. Miners work in horrendous climatic conditions in their search for precious gemstones. The sites are in my humble opinion hell holes, but people keep coming, hoping to strike it lucky. Typically, there is a significant transient population.

We spent 2 days in Lightning Ridge (NSW), home of the famous black opal, the most prized stone. They are called black, but they come in every colour of the rainbow. Their dark body tone makes the colours on the face of the opal appear rich and intense. They are found between 6 and 18 metres from the surface-deep enough to make their mining hard work. This is not an occupation for the faint-hearted.

Lighting Ridge offers a vision of gritty life in the Australian outback. It is like stepping onto a different planet. It is hot, dry and eerily still. Thank goodness for the water spa baths (artesian bore), which can provide some relief to aching muscles. We tried the one in Lightning Ridge, but it was so hot–nearly 40 degrees–that I almost fainted. We only stayed in for 10 minutes. Most visitors were just dangling their feet on the edge. Maybe that is the smartest thing to do as I came out as red as a lobster and not feeling well at all.

Pearls

The pearling industry in Western Australia had a dangerous beginning. Many people died in the pursuit of the precious pearls laying in the Indian Ocean. Walking through the streets of Broome, we were confronted with information signs that did not hide the ugly truth.

Pearls are found in oyster shells lined with a smooth coating of a material called 'nacre'. When something like a stone or grit gets inside the oyster shell, the oyster rids itself of the discomfort by coating the object with layer after layer of nacre, so that in time a pearl is formed. Pearl fishing as a money-making industry in the colony began in 1861. An early centre of the industry was at Cossack (WA) where we stayed for three days.

At first the oysters were gathered from the rocks or reefs, but that rapidly depleted stocks. The next step was to go find them in the sea. Aboriginal people who were known to be good swimmers were used as slave labour–a practice known as 'blackbirding'. They worked from small boats, diving into the water naked except for string bags around their waists. The majority of the divers were women, who were better than men at this work. Many divers died due to disease, shark attacks, cyclones and maltreatment. During the 1870's, the 'employment' of Aboriginal people was discouraged. The government passed regulations to protect them and forbade the use of women as divers. Better late than never, I suppose.

Malay and Japanese men replaced them. The conditions were harsh and the death rate high. Diving was brutally exhausting work. During the 1880's, diving suits were introduced so that oyster gathering could go on in deeper water. Another problem appeared: the 'bends' caused by diving too deep and coming up too fast. The human body cannot handle it. At depth, nitrogen from the air is dissolved in the blood. This causes the divers' blood to 'boil' as the nitrogen is expelled in a froth of bubbles. The diver either dies or is crippled for the rest of his life. Today the aqualung has replaced the cumbersome diving suit and now divers can be saved from the bends by being placed in a decompression chamber. There are fewer incidents in the industry today. Broome was reportedly the first place in Australia to have a decompression chamber, which has saved many lives over the years.

The boats used for pearling were called 'pearling luggers' and were unique to Australia. By 1910, nearly 400 pearling luggers and more than 3,500 people were fishing for shell around Broome, making it the world's largest pearling centre. We went for a sunset cruise on *Willie*, the last operating pearl lugger in Australia. Willie is a 67-foot Gaff Rig Schooner and was built in 1985. There is no nasty history attached to it. Willie has been operating as a tourist vessel since 2019.

Thankfully, Australia's pearling industry is mostly based now on the cultivation of pearls. Divers collect pearl oysters and bring them to oyster farms. A bead is implanted into each oyster, and the oysters are put back in the water. The beads encourage the oysters to form pearls, which are harvested to make jewellery. Broome continues to be a world leader in the production of South Sea pearls.

CHAPTER 33

Who had that bright idea?

I HAVE THE UTMOST RESPECT for engineers. I studied mining and geological engineering at Universite Laval in Quebec City for 18 months. I never finished the 3-year degree after the biggest romantic heartbreak of my life. Fate took me in a different direction, and I moved away. But I often wonder what my life would have been like if I had finished that degree. Witnessing firsthand the impressive work done by engineers in this country leaves me in total admiration of their great minds. The first project that impressed me no end was in Western Australia.

Ord River Irrigation Scheme (ORIS)

We were lucky to fly over a small section of the Ord (WA), which is a 65-kilometre-long river in the Kimberley region. The immensity of the project can only be appreciated from the air. The idea of damming the Ord was first mentioned over 100 years ago, but it took a while to come to fruition. The surrounding area is desert-like, and it seemed far-fetched to imagine tropical agriculture developing there. But between 1935 and 1942, drought affected the Kimberley pastoral industry and that formed the impetus for the Ord Scheme.

Water is diverted from Lake Kununurra and is gravity fed through a series of open channels to farms. The water is used to grow a variety of agricultural crops, including mango, citrus, watermelon, rockmelon, pumpkin, chickpea, bananas and chia. It is home to the largest commercial Indian Sandalwood plantation in the world.

In 1963, the Kununurra Diversion Dam was built, marking completion of the first stage of the Ord Irrigation Scheme. This investment also led to the establishment of the town of Kununurra, built as the service centre for the scheme. Lake Argyle was created in 1972 to support irrigation expansion and is the largest freshwater storage on mainland Australia. Its storage capacity is nearly 20 times the water volume of Sydney Harbour, which is really saying something.

ORIS continues to expend with more land being released for agriculture. All the neat rectangular green fields, full of goodness growing for our tables, were an amazing sight to see from the air. But much of the produce is exported to Southeast Asia.

The Ord River dams provide water for the irrigation of over 117 square kilometres of farmland, and extensions to the scheme are underway to allow for a further 440 square kilometres. The main Ord River dam also generates hydro power for the local community of Kununurra.

The Golden Pipeline

We followed the whole length of this incredible project called The Golden Pipeline from Mundaring Weir to Kalgoorlie (WA). I can report that it is not made of gold nor is it golden. It was named 'Golden' because of gold found in Kalgoorlie. The Golden Pipeline Heritage trail took us on an unforgettable journey.

We learned that the scheme delivers water to Western Australia's Eastern goldfields, rich in the precious metal but lacking in an even more precious resource: fresh water. Water from Mundaring Dam near Perth is lifted by a series of 8 pump stations through a steel pipeline to its destination 560 kilometres east. It is an engineering marvel with the saddest human tragedy attached to it and possibly the first recorded case of bullying with a tragic ending.

At the time of its construction (1898–1902) many thought the scheme would fail. It was the persistence of engineer CY O'Connor and Premier John Forrest that made it happen.

Charles Yelverton (CY) O'Connor was an Irishman who spent 26 years working in New Zealand before coming to Western Australia in 1891. Premier John Forrest appointed him to oversee 'railways, harbours, everything'. CY O'Connor proposed a pumping scheme to solve the shortage of fresh water in the Eastern Goldfields. He worked on the project for four years.

Many parliamentarians strongly opposed the scheme due to the high cost and predicted uselessness. They called it a 'scheme of madness'. A Royal Commission was set up in early 1902 to enquire into accusations of mismanagement. It was based on false allegations that O'Connor was corrupt. He trusted his own engineering judgement was sound, but he was deeply hurt by the suggestions that he was dishonest. He took his own life five days after the Royal Commission began taking evidence and only three weeks before No. 1 pump station began operating.

On 24 January 1903, Sir John Forrest officially opened the Goldfields Water Supply Scheme in Kalgoorlie, expressing his sadness that O'Connor had not lived to receive the honour so justly due to him.

Today an 8,000 kilometres network of pipes radiates north and south of the original west–east pipeline. The scheme was built when 30,000 people resided in the goldfields. These days 100,000 people rely on it. It guarantees a secure water supply for those living in the Wheatbelt that supplies half of the nation's wheat and millions of sheep.

CY O'Connor had an unfortunate early demise, but his legacy is unsurpassed.

Lennox Bridge

We were fortunate to drive over the oldest stone arch bridge on the mainland. Actually, we almost did not make it as a sign up the hill stated that the bridge was restricted to vehicles less than 5 tonnes. The Golden Goose is 5.3 tonnes. It was a tense moment, but the bridge did not collapse. Our nervous systems almost did!

Lennox Bridge is in Glenbrook (NSW). It is a heritage-listed road bridge over Lapstone Creek. The bridge was named after David Lennox who designed and built it between 1832 and 1833. Lennox was not an engineer but a stonemason from Scotland. The stone arch bridge is a single arch of six metres span with a road width of nine metres. The small bridge, on a horseshoe curve, was daring for its time and remarkably attractive.

David Lennox worked with convicts who had suitable experience. They opened a quarry near the creek and cut the stone blocks right there. The keystones have engraved on them on the south side 'DAVID LENNOX', while on the north side they have 'AD 1833'.

The road is now one way only downhill from Lennox Bridge and the traffic is largely for tourist purposes. There is a small car parking space beside the bridge and a concrete stairwell and path down to the creek. We parked the Goose and walked under the bridge to view the intricate stonework up close. It is charming if you ignore the modern graffiti on it.

Lennox Bridge is exceptional. No other bridges of similar age or design have survived on the mainland. The bridge received a Historic Engineering Marker from Engineers Australia in 2001.

CHAPTER 34

How big are the farms?

I HAVE STARTED THINKING OF Australia as a big patchwork quilt with a red centre. It certainly looks like one from above with all the big rectangular patches of different colours. They are fields of distinct crops. We are so lucky to grow so much of our food in this mostly arid country. It is due in many cases to irrigation schemes like the one mentioned earlier in the Ord region of Western Australia.

Agriculture accounts for over half of Australia's land use and it occurs mostly on the coast. Wheat is by far the largest crop, followed by barley, canola, cotton and sugar. Of course, we also grow fruit and vegetables. Over 90 percent of all fresh vegetables sold in Australian supermarkets are grown here. Small family farms still exist, but more than 60 percent of production is dominated by large farms that grow over 70 hectares of vegetables. They are the big patches on the 'quilt'.

Wheat

Sting's famous song *'Fields of Gold'* ran through my head as we drove past endless yellow fields of wheat. We noticed that the wheat stalks were shorter than we remembered. No, we were not dreaming. Scientists have developed through genetic mutations a dwarf variety of wheat that requires less water. Plants with shorter stems are less likely to fall over during windy days and as a result greater yields are harvested. However, shorter stalks mean less sun and shallower roots systems, leading to lower levels of many vitamins and minerals. Modern wheat is lower in zinc, magnesium, iron, copper, and selenium than its ancient ancestor. I feel ancient remembering the taller wheat!

Wheat is the second-most-produced cereal grain after maize, and the global trade of wheat is greater than all other crops combined. Everybody likes bread, pasta, pizza and noodles!

Australia is the world's sixth largest wheat exporter. It supplies mainly China, Indonesia, and Japan.

Cotton

We drove to northern New South Wales while the cotton fields were in full bloom. I don't know why the sight of millions of fluffy white bolls of cotton got me so excited. I just had to get out of the bus and go touch them. I might have been trespassing, but I had to see them up close. I could not resist picking a little bunch. They were so soft. So now I am a trespasser and a thief. Somehow, I don't think the farmer will miss three bolls of cotton. The boll is the fruit of the plant.

Australia is a relatively minor producer on the world scale but is the world's third-to-sixth largest exporter depending on the season. Our 1,500 cotton farms produce enough cotton to clothe on average 500 million people per year. The farms are mostly in New South Wales and Queensland. Our exports go principally to China, Bangladesh, Vietnam, India, and Indonesia. Growing cotton in Australia is a highly controversial topic. Cotton needs a lot of water, and we are living in the lowest rainfall continent on Earth. How does that work?

About 90 percent of Australia's cotton crop is irrigated. This changes every year depending on how much natural rainfall is received across the cotton-growing catchments. The human management of rivers, such as the allocation of water for irrigation and other uses, is a touchy subject in this country. Some say Australia was never meant to grow cotton. But the cotton industry's long-term monitoring seems to demonstrate that cotton farms have significantly improved their water efficiency over time.

Another argument is that water is not allocated to crops but to a farmer's licence. The farmer chooses what they want to use their allocated water on. If cotton was banned, there would not be one more drop of water in our rivers because farmers would use the water to grow something else. Cotton is only planted once a year in Australia, and only when there is enough water available. With the recent droughts and flood events, there has been less cotton grown.

Sugar cane

The sugar cane industry has a shocking past. Sugarcane was brought to Australia in 1788 on the First Fleet. It was not immediately successful as the first settlers foolishly attempted to grow the cane in Macquarie (NSW). The first viable cane plantation was established near Brisbane in 1862 where the climate was better suited. Two years later the first commercial sugar mill was built.

Australia's sugarcane is grown in high rainfall and irrigated areas along coastal plains and river valleys on 2,100 kilometres of Australia's eastern coastline, mostly in Queensland.

But back to the beginning when white settlers developed sugarcane plantations in the tropics. The Queensland Government were keen to support their endeavours, to increase income and trade in the colony. Everything was functioning well due to the cheap manpower provided by convicts. But when convict transportation stopped, who else was there to take on the back-breaking job? White men didn't have the strength to work in the ferocious tropical climate, and on top of that they felt that it was beneath them.

The devious thought of free black labour was born. Magically the source for that labour was next door in Vanuatu, the Solomon

Islands and the New Hebrides. An estimated 62,500 Islanders were brought to Queensland between 1863 and 1904.

While most Islanders came voluntarily, some were brought over illegally, having been kidnapped or 'blackbirded'. Other Islanders were persuaded to leave their homes and travel by ship to Queensland by coercion, force or deception. Islanders who came to Australia on recruitment ships were usually contracted or 'indentured' for three years. Some eventually stayed permanently in Australia. This suggests some recruits had decided life in Australia was better than returning to their homeland.

Australia is the second largest raw sugar exporter in the world with China, South Korea, Indonesia, Japan, and Malaysia being our major clients.

Wind

I know wind is not food, but it is 'farmed'. I have to talk about the wind farms because we saw so many. It seemed like they were around every corner. At the last count, there are 98 wind farms located throughout all states. Wind power is the cheapest source of large-scale renewable energy. Hence, there are more wind farms being built as I write this. This is a fast-growing industry. This is not surprising considering that Australia has some of the best wind resources in the world. The winds are blowing mainly in the southern parts of the mainland, right in the path of the 'roaring 40s'.

Most of the onshore farms are far away in the distance, and you see the massive turbines appear on the horizon as you drive. Our first up-close encounter was at Walkaway (WA). There was a place to pull up and read information panels. The most interesting thing was a *huge* old turbine blade resting on supporting concrete blocks. We parked the Goose right next to it to appreciate its size. The photo is not an optical illusion. That blade is 52 metres long; the bus is just over seven metres!

HOW BIG ARE THE FARMS?

Walkaway Wind Farm is located 30 kilometres south-east of Geraldton (WA) and 12 kilometres inland from the Indian Ocean. This is one of the windiest regions in Australia. Wind speeds average 20–25 kilometres per hour during the cooler months and 25–35 kilometres per hour from October to March. The wind turbines occupy less than one percent of farmland within the site, allowing stock grazing and broad acreage cropping to continue.

It is the second biggest wind farm in Western Australia. It comprises 54 wind turbines and has been operating since 2006. This wind farm generates enough power for approximately 64,000 homes and each turbine produces carbon savings exceeding those used during its production within four months of commencing generation.

CHAPTER 35

Anyone for a glass of wine?

WE LIKE A DROP OF fermented grape juice with our meals on special occasions. But I was never a fine wine connoisseur. I had limited knowledge of the wine industry. I had picked grapes in the Burgundy region of France in 1984 for two weeks and the work was backbreaking. I had visited Australian wineries before, of course, particularly in the Hunter Valley when I lived on the New South Wales Central Coast. But the industry there was relatively young. It sure had changed when I returned 30 years later.

The trip exposed me to such a variety of wine regions, and I learned so much from the knowledgeable independent winemakers. I have refined my palate and now drink three sips before I judge if I like the wine or not. A trick I picked up somewhere in Western Australia. But I still go with my taste buds and how much I like the label.

We know people who travel exclusively to visit wineries and cellar doors. We saw them sniffing, swirling and spitting in buckets. We are not judgemental and each to their own. We were just a little more casual in our tastings. For us, it was just something else to look at and try. We love food and liquids that go with it. We did find our preferred experiences involved beautiful scenery overlooking the vineyards, a wine paddle with the tasting notes and Watson being allowed to sit next to us. We did not like sitting at a pop-up cellar door in town, which happened on a wine tour in Margaret River, Western Australia. I think they are missing the point of the whole sensory extravaganza. It has tainted our memory of that region, which many people laud as the best wine growing area in Australia.

But let us look at the wine industry in more detail. The favourable climate of the land down under and rich soil to grow the best grapes have turned this into big business.

Vineyards cover a massive area of which South Australia accounts for 52 percent, New South Wales 24 percent and Victoria 15 percent. The most popular varietals are shiraz (25 percent) and chardonnay (21 percent). Shiraz is too strong for my taste. I had given up chardonnay after possibly drinking too much of it in the 1980s, wooded and unwooded.

Australia is one of the world's largest wine exporters, mostly to the USA. The numbers are staggering with nearly 800 million out of the 1.2 to 1.3 billion litres produced annually exported to overseas markets. That still leaves a fair bit for Australians. Apparently, we like drinking our own wines and we buy more domestic wines than imported ones. Cheers to that!

Wine is produced in every state and there are now more than 60 designated wine regions. There are over 2,100 wineries and around 6,000 grape growers. I don't think anyone could live long enough to visit all the wineries even if that is all their holidays revolved around.

We managed to visit 7 regions: Margaret River (WA), Barossa Valley (SA), Clare Valley (SA), McLaren Valley (SA), Riverland (SA), Langhorn (SA) and Hunter Valley (NSW).

The Barossa Valley, South Australia

Our favourite by far was the Barossa Valley (SA). It is where I saw and photographed my first gnarled old vines, and what a sight they were. They were planted in 1894 by German immigrants, the Scholz, on the banks of the North Para River.

The Barossa is home to *the oldest vines in the world*, born in 1843 at Langmeil Winery in Tanunda. I could not understand why such a young country as Australia would have the oldest vines. I then learned that they are descendants of the first vine collection brought to Australia by James Busby in 1832 from the heartland of France, the Rhone Valley. Unfortunately, their French ancestors were completely wiped out when phylloxera, an insect pest, decimated the vineyards of Europe 50 years later. That pest did not visit our shores, so these early Australian vine plantings are irreplaceable.

But what insects could not destroy, the terrible bushfires of 2019–20 did. Fire destroyed up to 30 percent of the vineyards. The rest of the grapes were smoke tainted. Many wineries were just getting back on their feet when we visited in 2023.

Yalumba Winery

This winery will always stand out in our mind, not for the wine which we never tasted (it was too early in the day) but for the cooperage visit. What is wine without an oak barrel to mature in? Yalumba claims to be the only winery in the Southern Hemisphere to have had an operational, on-site cooperage since 1890. They employ two full-time coopers. We did not see them in action making barrels when we visited as harvesting had not started yet. But the workshop was open, and we were fortunate enough to be allowed in. We learned all about the process with many informative panels displayed around the huge shed. It is a fascinating craft and a serious science. I don't believe there is much fun in rolling out the barrels in the cooperage: just hard work and much dedication.

Small Victories Winery

The Small Victories Winery offered us the most unusual wine tasting experience ever. First, we were the only patrons there on that sunny day, sitting in the shade overlooking old vines. Watson was sitting at our feet getting lots of pats from the friendly and attentive staff. The wine tasting included four wines with matched *potato chips* for textural contrast. I had learned years ago from my French friends that you could drink champagne with salted chips (or thin biscuits, as in the Rhone valley). I tried it and liked it. I had never really pursued it any further. We seized this opportunity to explore the combination of easy drinking wines and crispy goodness: a genial marketing idea. It was an explosion of flavours and textures in our mouths. I highly recommend that you send your taste buds on an adventure of their own and visit this winery.

McLaren Vale, South Australia

We loved the scenery 45 minutes south of Adelaide. It was so green and lush compared to where we had come from, which had been so red and dry. The McLaren Vale wine region hosts around 80 wineries. It's in the heart of the Fleurieu Peninsula between the Gulf of St Vincent and Mount Lofty Ranges. If you don't like wine, you can simply soak up the colourful vistas. But if you do like wine, then you will be very happy.

D'Arenberg Winery

I already talked about the amazing Cube at D'Arenberg and the winemaker genius Chester Osborn in a previous chapter. Now I want to mention the actual wine tasting. Since 1912, the Osborn family have grown grapes and made wine in the picturesque surrounds of McLaren Vale. The wines have the most unusual names that make you reach for your dictionary such as: the Apotropaic Triskaidekaphobia, the Piceous Lodestar, the Pickwickian

Brobdingnagian, the Vociferate Dipsomaniac and my personal favourite the Cenosilicaphobic Cat. So, the wines and their names are a good mouthful.

The tasting room is on the fourth floor of the Cube. We had spectacular views while we sipped our wines. It was a civilised affair as we had pre-booked our tasting experience. Our wine waiter welcomed us and gave us full attention. The wines selected for tasting were very nice and we went home with a few bottles.

We then had the most mouth-watering lunch in the funkiest mad-hatter-themed restaurant you can ever imagine. It is called The Singapore Circus. It truly is an over-the-top sensory show. The cuisine is a fusion of southeast dishes, and it was all delicious. I would go back there in a heartbeat. It was one of the highlights of the trip.

Riverland, South Australia

We discovered the Riverland area by pure chance as we were just following the Murray River as far as we could. The Riverland produces some 460,000 tonnes of grapes and more than 85 varietals, making it a significant part of the Australian wine industry. In fact, by volume the Riverland produces most of the wine from South Australia. We were simply driving along when we were faced with gigantic buildings on either side of the road at Berri. What were we looking at?

Berri Estate Winery

Berri Estate winery is the largest grape processor in the Southern Hemisphere, crushing around 220,000 tonnes of grapes annually: around a third of South Australia's entire crush. The facility exports over 100 million litres of wine around the world annually. Wrap your mind around these numbers: over six and a half million litres of wine are delivered to the UK every month! What we saw from the road was only a fraction of the mammoth storage capacity of over 263 million litres, with 1,500 tanks on site and three automated production lines. Berri is the capital of cask wine with production of up to 85,000 casks a day. They come in all sizes, many of which we didn't know existed. I had bought the odd 2-litre and 4-litre casks when desperate in my younger years. But we now know that wine comes also in 1.5-, 3-, 5-, 10- and even 20-litre casks for commercial use.

CHAPTER 36

Is it a pub or a hotel?

I AM STILL NOT SURE of the difference between a pub and a hotel. In my mind, pubs were dingey and hotels classier. But I can tell you now that I have seen classy pubs and dingey hotels.

An Australian pub (short for public house) is an establishment licensed to serve alcoholic drinks. They may also provide entertainment, meals and basic accommodation. You could call them hotels. The Australian pub is a cultural icon and has always been more than just a place to drink. It is the vital centre of social life for some people. Every little town has a pub or two.

The Australian pub is a direct descendant of the English and Irish pub. However, in the nineteenth century the local version evolved several distinctive features that set it apart from its UK cousins. Often, pubs were the first structures built in newly colonised areas especially on the goldfields. By contrast, it was churches in Canada, would you believe. Pubs served many functions: hostelry, post office, restaurant, meeting place and even general store. There are now more than 6,000 pubs and bars in Australia. You cannot be thirsty for too long here.

I am not really a pub person. I don't even drink beer. Of course, they sell other drinks but cold beer on tap is what pubs are famous for, especially in this dry land. Nevertheless, on our travels we found some watering holes to be quite appealing.

Middleton Hotel

Middleton Hotel is a 'must-stop' when travelling from Boulia to Winton on the back roads. It is 170 kilometres from the nearest town with the unique distinction of being one of the most isolated pubs in Queensland. Middleton has a population of four people: basically, the couple who owns the hotel and their two young children.

This settlement made history in 1862 when McKinlay and his search party for Burke and Wills explored the area. It became Middleton in 1876 and a hotel was built. It was a Cobb & Co changing station until the service ceased in 1915. There is still an old Cobb & Co coach outside stranded there forever. The town that grew up around the hotel has since long gone without a trace. There is now only the hotel.

The scenery however is spectacular. The Cawnpore Lookout nearby will take your breath away. We stayed there for one night and we had it all to ourselves. The 'Hilton Hotel' across from the pub offers free accommodation. The name is quintessential Queenslander humour at its best. You see, it's actually a campground.

We had a drink at the pub, a good look around at the artifacts and moved on.

IS IT A PUB OR A HOTEL?

Palace Hotel

The Palace Hotel in Kalgoorlie (WA) is a majestic building. We had dinner at the Irish Bar on one side of the building. But we were flabbergasted by what we found at the main entrance to the hotel on the other side. The most atrocious yet beguiling massive mirror stood before us. It had been given to the hotel as a farewell gift by a very famous patron. Next to it was a framed poem by Herbert Hoover dedicated to a local barmaid, or so the story goes. Before he was the US President, Herbert Hoover was a 23-year-old mining engineer working in Kalgoorlie mines. He was a regular guest of this grand old gold rush hotel. Apparently, nothing came out of his extravagant gift, and he just went on with his destiny.

The authorship of the poem has been disputed. Hoover had been brought up as a Quaker and was engaged to be married, which he did as soon as he returned home. Given the morals of the time, it is unlikely that he would have had a relationship with a barmaid. But was that not a titillating story, nevertheless?

Carinda Hotel

We made a huge detour to visit the Carinda Hotel in central New South Wales. It was over 60 kilometres of badly sealed road, but we were on a mission. You see, the Carinda Hotel is sacred ground for David Bowie fans. It is where he filmed parts of his music video for '*Let's Dance*', the 1983 disco hit. It put Carinda on the international map. The 1930's pub is nothing to look at inside and out. They have a life-size photo of David Bowie standing near the wall just like in the video. They have placed a small table and a vase with plastic flowers near it as some sort of shrine. David Bowie as a semi-god: we worshipped at his altar. It is all quite bizarre and anti-climactic when you get there. But we took the tourist photos: we just had to. We spent the night at the free camping on the showgrounds.

Since David Bowie's passing in 2016, the town has hosted an annual celebration of all things Bowie in their Let's Dance Carinda event in October long weekend. Mark your calendars!

IS IT A PUB OR A HOTEL?

The Dromedary Hotel

Another serendipitous finding when we were looking for the cheese factory in Tilba was the Dromedary Hotel. This gorgeous old country pub, dating from 1895, is in the beautiful National Trust village of Central Tilba, on the far south coast of New South Wales. It is the oldest timber pub in Australia. The whole village consists of timber buildings and it is so quaint and cute.

Reportedly, the 'Drom' was built from wood recycled from the whaling ships that docked at Bermagui Harbour. It was not originally a pub, but rather a coffee place named the Palace Hotel. The name changed to Hotel Dromedary in 1936 after nearby Mount Dromedary.

We saw so many plaques on hotel walls describing how many times the original timber hotels had burnt down and been replaced by a modern concrete version. We were astounded that this hotel had survived that long when it is surrounded by forests: a miracle! They have a beautiful beer garden out the back and live music. A great trio was playing the Sunday afternoon we were there. The service was friendly and the food excellent.

Tattersalls Hotel

We love Art Deco and fortunately saw many Art Deco pubs with spectacular facades. The most impressive was the Tattersalls Hotel.

This hotel was established in 1858 in Armidale (NSW) as the Wellington Inn. In 1873, the hotel was demolished to make room for a new 3-storey Wellington Hotel. It opened in May 1874 and was reportedly the 'best Hotel in the north of New South Wales'. Ten years later a new owner changed the name to the Tattersalls Hotel. There were many more changes of ownership and renovations. In 1936, the hotel was remodelled in the fashion of the day, Art Deco style.

The hotel had a major renovation in 2016. The new owners have kept to the original design with upgrades of luxury and sophistication. They must have had a huge budget. All three floors were gutted to allow for the creation of 25 guest rooms and suites. The original facades were conserved, as were interior features such as a glass skylight, pressed tin ceilings and solid timber-lined stairways, restored to former glory with rich walnut stains. The entire hotel was equipped with bespoke Art Deco fittings, furniture and even carpets. They have a small museum on the first floor, which we visited. We felt we were not dressed well enough to have a meal in the grand dining room. But we wanted to, so badly! The menu was tempting and the décor to die for. We are planning to come back soon dressed in 1920's clothes.

CHAPTER 37

Isn't that beautiful?

THE AUSTRALIAN FLORA WAS A never-ending source of astonishment with plenty of 'oos and aas'. I had not realised how many different types of native flowers and trees there are here until I went around Australia. Would you believe there are over 25,000 species of flowering plants? This kind of abundance is only found in Australia and South Africa. There are so many they cannot possibly be all named. I like to label things and know the names of flowers. I thought I had hit the jackpot when I bought a field guide with Western Australian flowers classified in colour coding–how clever! It contained only 400 photos–a drop in the ocean of flowers we spotted. Most of the flowers we saw were not in that book. In the end, I was just happy to look at their beauty and be spellbound by the diversity of colours and shapes. A treasure chest! I took hundreds of photos.

Western Australia on its own has over 12,000 species. The wildflower season occurs each year from July to October and is deemed one of the top botanical wonders of the world. Over the years, I had seen many advertisements on the east coast for organised trips to see that wonderful spectacle of Mother Nature. I was always tempted to go, but the high price had always stopped me

THE EDUCATIONAL JOURNEY

from booking a seat. But with our 'Goose' we could finally see the spring festival.

The flowers start blooming north of Geraldton in July and slowly progress south. We left home in July and only got to Geraldton at the end of October, very late in the season. Nonetheless, we saw infinite fields of flowers by the side of the road. The national parks were tapestries of blooms and buzzing bees. And because we were travelling from north to south, we kept seeing them, to our amazement. I can only imagine now what the show would be like in the peak of the season.

The flowers on show will change from year to year depending on the rainfall and the weather. Of course, I had a few favourites.

The first time I saw Mulla Mullas, I was super thrilled because they looked so different. Those lilac-coloured conical flowers are low to the ground. It was near Lake Dunn (QLD) only eight days after leaving Brisbane. Apparently, the heavy floods preceding our arrival had made them explode and they were everywhere. Mulla Mulla normally flowers in spring but it was still winter. They are perennials that grow in harsh environments such as the stony plains of the Outback. But we kept bumping into varieties of them all the way to Western Australia and I never tired of seeing them.

ISN'T THAT BEAUTIFUL?

Look at them just growing on stones or rocky cliffs.

THE EDUCATIONAL JOURNEY

My other favourite was the Sturt's desert pea, another tough flower that thrives on neglect in the arid plains. It is a weird looking plant to be honest. It has a unique blood-red, leaf-like flower, each with a bulbous black centre. To me it looks like aliens with black eyes staring at me. It is one of Australia's best known wildflowers and grows everywhere on the mainland except in Victoria.

CHAPTER 38

Does it bite?

I LOVE ANIMALS SO MUCH that I studied at college for two years to get a certificate in veterinary nursing. Moreover, dogs are my favourite domesticated animals, and I studied another 18 months to get my qualifications in Dog Behaviour Training. But nothing beats seeing wild animals in their natural habitat. I went to Africa in 2011 specifically to see their incredible fauna. But Australia's fauna is unique because the island has been geographically isolated for so long. Our fauna consists of a large variety of animals: birds, mammals, amphibians, and reptiles that can be found nowhere else in the world.

Birds

I love birds so much that we have a whole room in our house dedicated to birds. The walls are covered in paintings and photos. There are shelves with sculptures, figurines, and lamps. Even when I am unconscious, I think about birds: one of my recurring dreams is that I am flying like a bird, flapping my arms like wings.

There are over 900 recorded species of Australian birds, and some are very elusive. But one species in particular we found everywhere: the **emu.** We spotted families with young chicks by the side of the road and learned that they like the beach. We saw one in front of our motorhome on Fowler's Beach (WA) just walking in the shallows. At some point, it jumped back in fright having encountered something scary underwater that we could not identify. I have it on video, and it still makes me laugh to watch it! We saw three emus rummaging for food in a caravan park in Monkey Mia (WA). There were signs everywhere not to leave anything outside for the birds to eat. Some people did not get the memo or chose to ignore it at their peril.

We saw emus in the wheatfields popping their heads up and down in a comedy routine like no other. But what I found funny is not funny to farmers. You see, the emu is the largest native bird in Australia: up to two metres in height and they weigh from 31 to 48 kilograms. It sometimes tramples crops, and it is thus classed as an agricultural pest in Western Australia. There was even a great Emu War in 1932 when the army was called in to cull emus on farms. But the emus put up a fight against the soldiers. It was estimated that it took 10 bullets to bring down every emu–a pretty dismal effort for trained army men. The government then decided to provide the ammunition directly to the farmers to take care of the problem themselves. It was a massacre: in 1941 over 57,000 emu lives were claimed in 6 months. It is ironic that the gangly bird is now a protected species and proudly displayed on the Australian coat of arms.

Black cockatoos are impressive birds of incredible beauty. I saw flocks of yellow-tailed black cockatoos flying out of their trees at sunbreak over my head in a cacophony of mournful wailing calls and screeches. They unfortunately do not have a melodious voice. But I don't hold that against them. I saw dozens of red-tailed black cockatoos shredding treetops and leaving a mess underneath. They can be very destructive.

Another species of black bird I adore is the **black swan**. Western Australia has plenty of black swans to swoon over. They are so graceful. And definitely sound better than the cockatoos, with a musical sound rather like a bugle.

The **Gouldian finch is** a most colourful little bird. Interestingly, both sexes are brightly covered with black, green, yellow, purple, and red markings. They have a paint job like a hot rod car: it's just crazy. It is hard to take a photo of them as they fly so fast out of sight.

I managed to take a few photos of the magnificent **blue fairy wren** when resting on a branch. I was drawn to its lovely high-pitched trills.

The **Australian ringneck parrot** was another little beauty flying here and there in Western Australia. They are also called 'twenty-eight parrot' because they sound like they are saying 'twenty-eight'!

But my all-time favourite bird is the **kookaburra**. Not only is it a beautiful bird of the kingfisher family, but it also makes the most contagious laughing sound in the animal kingdom. It always makes me smile to hear one in the bush.

THE EDUCATIONAL JOURNEY

Mammals

My encounters with mammals were always a delight. We have 357 native species of mammals in Australia. The most famous are undoubtedly the monotremes and marsupials. We saw three **echidnas** on the trip, and it was always a great thrill to spot one. They are so elusive.

We tried really hard to see a platypus in the wild but to no avail.

The **quokkas** of Rottnest Island are definitely the cutest marsupials and seem happy to see you. There are 10,000 on the island, so you are guaranteed to see them. They are famous for their friendliness and goofy smile as people take selfies next to them. I did not get a prize-winning photo, but it was good enough for me!

We saw hundreds of **kangaroos** and **wallabies**. Unfortunately, there were many dead ones by the side of the road, hit by passing cars and trucks. It is sad to report that we spotted a lot more dead wombats than live ones.

We saw **dugongs** in Shark Bay when we took a cruise. I did not take one single picture as they are so hard to pin down. But I was glad we saw them. Of course, we saw plenty of **dolphins**, but we have them at home too, so that was not overly exciting.

In Stansbury, South Australia, there was a big surprise as I was walking and taking photos: a huge **sea lion** was draped over the rocks on the jetty. It gave me such a start! I took a step back and managed to get a close-up photo.

In Portland, Victoria, we jumped on a boat tour to Seals Cave. Seeing thousands of **seals** in one place up close and engaging in their natural behaviours was thrilling. The cute pups were only three months old. They were like kids, running everywhere, pestering their elders, and occasionally having their behaviour corrected. It is the only mainland breeding colony of seals in Australia.

One lone **dingo** was walking calmly by the side of the highway, crossing the Nullarbor. He turned and stared as we drove by. I took a photo in one of those moments when time stops. We just looked at each other. And look how well they camouflage in the scenery.

Amphibians

I cannot pretend that seeing amphibians is as exciting as spotting birds and mammals. Nevertheless, they are part of our rich fauna and deserve a mention. The only amphibians we have in Australia are frogs. We have about 230 species of **native frogs** and unfortunately two invasive species: the **cane toad** and the **smooth newt.** Of course, we saw many lovely frogs. But the cane toads are something else. We have the dreadful cane toads in our own backyard in Queensland after heavy rains. I do not kill anything if I can avoid it. I even relocate spiders from inside the house to outside. But I cannot let cane toads go on reproducing. We give them a long rest in a freezer!

The cane toad is a large warty, poisonous amphibian native to South America. They came to Australia in 1935 at the request of sugarcane plantation owners in North Queensland. Over 2,000 were released in the hope that they would help control cane beetles. They have no natural predators in Australia, and they are rapidly spreading across our continent. They eat almost anything and reproduce easily. There are now 200 million cane toads in our country. It is a man-made ecological nightmare. Not only did they fail to control the cane beetles, but they also eat native animals such as small birds, other reptiles, amphibians and small mammals. To add insult to injury, the poisonous toads kill both pets (mostly dogs) and native species when the animals bite, lick, or eat them. The introduction of toads was a massive policy fail with ongoing repercussions. Even their eggs and tadpoles are toxic and can kill. That is one animal I hate the sight of.

Reptiles

I am not a big fan of reptiles either. Like many people, they scare me a little. But they can hardly be avoided in this country. Australia has a high diversity of reptiles, with over 830 species and 89 percent of those found nowhere else in the world. They include turtles, lizards, snakes and crocodiles. We saw plenty of turtles in

THE EDUCATIONAL JOURNEY

the sea and in fresh water. I like them. I don't mind lizards either; the blue tongue lizards are quite cute.

Cuteness is not a quality I would attribute to snakes. There are 188 species of snakes in Australia, including many venomous ones, but they are generally shy creatures. I can report that we never saw one snake in the whole trip. I am pretty sure they saw us.

The highlight for me in terms of reptiles was spotting a few freshwater crocodiles while on our Katherine Gorge cruise. There is something special about seeing a three-metre crocodile laying on the sandy shore or warming up on a rock. I was reassured that unlike the saltwater crocodiles, they are not aggressive and do not attack humans–usually.

Stromatolites

I have included stromatolites in this chapter, but they are neither a plant nor an animal. I had never heard of them before I saw them. But they are the oldest living form on Earth. They are not much to look at and I was initially underwhelmed. They are a cross between gigantic black cauliflowers and rocks. We thought they looked like big cow pats or large rotten molars!

Stromatolites are microbial reefs created by cyanobacteria, formerly known as blue-green algae. These tiny microbes are similar to organisms that existed 3.5 billion years ago. Earth itself has been around for 4.5 billion years. They are old indeed.

But there is an exciting part to this story: stromatolites are the reason why we are here today! Before cyanobacteria there was only one percent oxygen in the air. Then for two billion years, photosynthesising stromatolites pumped oxygen into the oceans. When the oceans' waters were saturated, oxygen was released into the air, and with around 20 percent of oxygen in the air, life was able to flourish and evolve. So, thank you stromatolites for your good work!

There are only two places on Earth where you can see them: in the Bahamas and at Hamelin Pool in the Shark Bay area of Western Australia. They are rare because they thrive in hypersaline water, twice as salty as normal seawater. We consider ourselves lucky to have seen them.

Due to their scarceness, they are protected from human interference. Visitors are restricted to a boardwalk normally. But we got there after a cyclone and the boardwalk was destroyed. That was disappointing as we only saw them from about 100 metres away. Maybe they are prettier than we thought when you get up close.

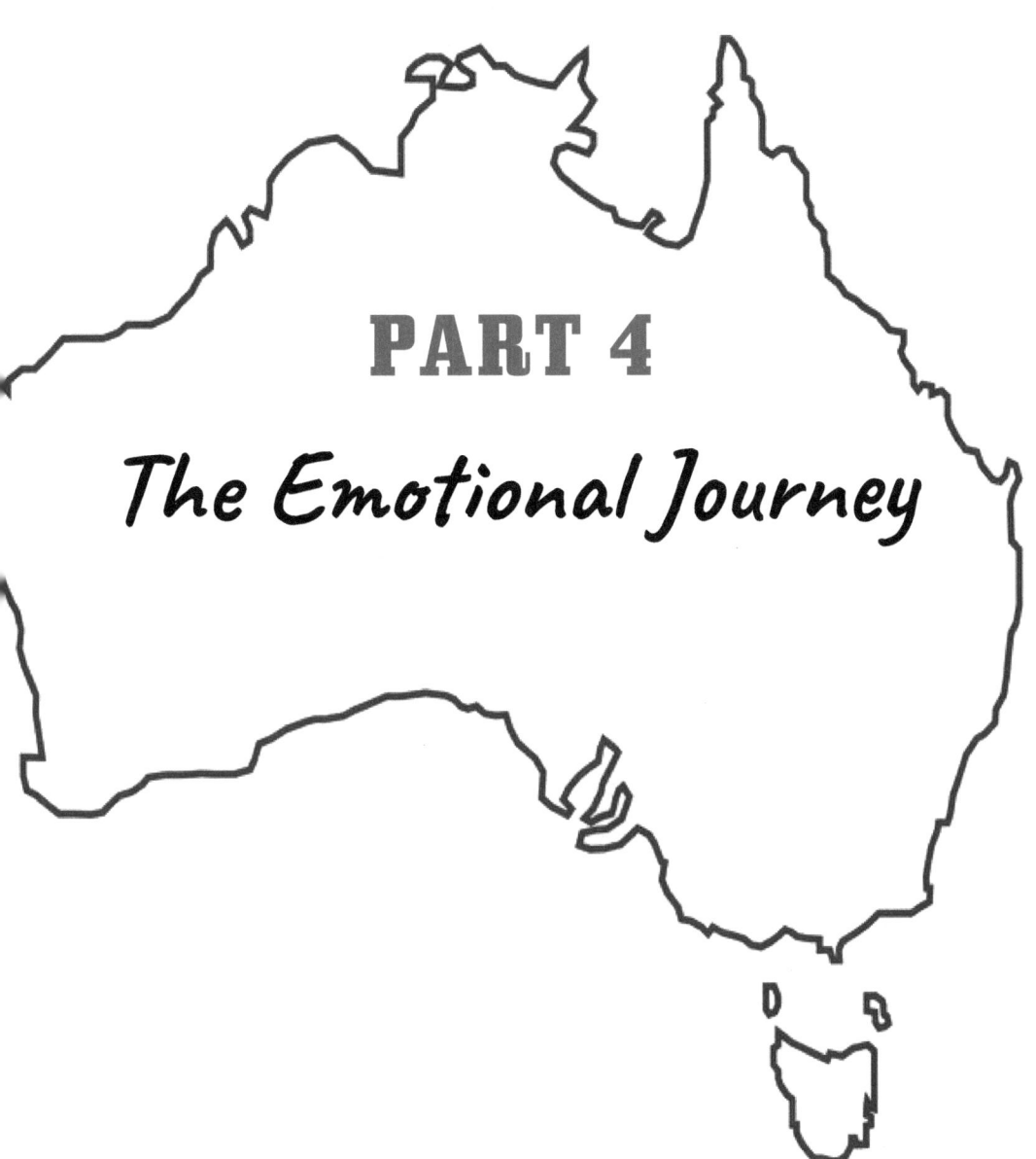

PART 4
The Emotional Journey

When you decide to leave everything familiar and embark on an epic tour of Australia, you have no idea what is ahead really. You make up some kind of story in your mind, with an imaginary sensory suite of sights, sounds, smells, tastes and touches. You don't consider really the full emotional impact of travelling. That just happens as you go along, just like in normal life. Except, nothing is normal anymore. You are totally out of your comfort zone and every day brings new challenges.

From the highest highs to the lowest lows, our moods changed continuously. Humans adapt to change amazingly well. We have had to, otherwise we would have become extinct a long time ago. But on a long journey, emotions were often raw as there was so much uncertainty surrounding us every day. You think you go on a trip and leave everything behind without a care in the world. You are 'living the dream'! You forget that you take your baggage with you everywhere you go.

The lap was an emotional rollercoaster due to internal and external factors. You read in the previous chapters how we were moved by the things we saw, read about and learned. They were the hidden secrets and tragedies of history that affected us one way or another. This chapter is about the internal factors that played on our heart strings.

CHAPTER 39

How did your couple survive?

THERE IS NO DENYING THAT living together in a small space for a long time is testing for any couple. I call it the 'sardine can syndrome'. I said to Chris when we were just planning the trip that this could make us or break us. Travelling brings out the best and the worst in people.

We both have had nightmarish experiences of travelling with previous partners on much shorter journeys. I was always much better at travelling alone. On my own, I could decide where to go, what to do, who to talk to and what to see. I could have my needs and my wants met without any hassles. I love solo travelling, and I did plenty of it over three decades.

Chris and I had travelled a lot together in the short 4.5 years we had been together. Of course, that included 2.5 years of COVID restrictions that seriously impacted our movements. We have been overseas twice: first to Europe in 2018 for our honeymoon then a trip to Canada in 2019 to introduce him to my family. That second trip included a cruise to Alaska. We have travelled extensively in Queensland with numerous excursions on our motorbikes. There were short getaways when we were both working full time. I can say that he is my best travelling companion by far.

THE EMOTIONAL JOURNEY

I would never have contemplated such a long trip with anyone but Chris. He is a practical man who can fix just about anything. He has an engineering background and a 'can do' attitude. He has over 40 years of experience exploring and adventuring in the great outback on his motorcycles. With his mate David, he has crossed the Simpson and Stony Deserts and explored Cape York and countless other inhospitable spots. Chris is smart and sensible and good at quick risk assessments. He is not afraid of getting his hands dirty. He is hard working. But best of all, he is a fantastic cook and makes me laugh no end. He truly is the best companion and husband for me.

Nevertheless, it was with some trepidation that we launched ourselves on our Big Lap. We knew this was a different kind of trip and that nothing could fully prepare us for it. We call ourselves 'team formidable', and this was a job to prove the team could do it!

A journey of a thousand miles starts with the first step. In our case, the first kilometre of driving was when we decided that Chris would be the main driver because he is a much more experienced driver and I hate driving. I am however a natural navigator with a good sense of orientation. I am also a trained navigator from my years in the Canadian Coast Guard. On our trip, I relied on Google Maps, our Australian Atlas, a GPS and tourist brochures collected along the way to guide us from place to place. They worked well for most of the journey. But sometimes we had no reception on our mobile phones and totally no idea where we were. The scale in our Atlas was too small, signs on the road had often disappeared or been removed on purpose (or shot out!) and some points of interest were so elusive! Most of our disagreements were related to driving and navigation.

I do not have a short fuse and it takes a lot to make me angry. I can normally hold it together when faced with difficult situations. But even the most patient of souls will eventually lose control in a spectacular fashion.

When my navigation was a point of contention, I would swap roles with Chris so that he could experience the challenges for himself. But I was then faced with a new problem: the critique of my driving abilities. Driving a small bus is not that hard, yet it was a new experience for me. I believe I can drive the Golden Goose as well as Chris does, but at times he did not approve of my driving. That would lead to tense moments and occasional harsh words. I do not respond well to a raised voice and an angry tone. That is one trigger that turns me into an unpredictable woman.

The first episode was less than two weeks into the trip. On reflection, there was so much to absorb about the management of the Goose. The steep learning curve of figuring out where to go each day was adding to the stress. A perfect storm was brewing, and it all came to a head in Winton, Queensland. Chris said something about my driving in an unkind manner. I stopped the bus and jumped out.

I walked away slamming the door behind me. I was furious. I had just the clothes on my back and nothing else. I walked aimlessly around the main street, stopped in a public toilet and had a good cry. I felt very sorry for myself. But I eventually calmed down and returned to the bus, which Chris had parked in a visible spot. Then we followed our secret formula.

Whenever we have issues, we do a relationship repair technique in three steps:

1. Acknowledge what went wrong.
2. Ask for forgiveness. (Do not say 'I am sorry' but 'Will you forgive me?')
3. Ask genuinely 'How can I make it better?'

I can't recall where I got that from, but I have been using this process for years. None of us is perfect. We are all humans trying our best to improve: we are works of art in progress.

The second episode was near the end of the trip funnily enough. I think I just had enough by then and was fraying at the edges. The toll of constantly moving from one place to another was a factor. The sudden drop in temperature in Central New South Wales was another. I hate the cold! I left Canada because I could not stand it. The ongoing discussions about navigation and where to go next were accumulating. Just one look at the zig zagging on the map in New South Wales will show how erratic our trip had become. We were both exhausted by the sheer physical effort of moving so often. I lost the plot in Armidale after one last laundry trip. I exploded in anger. Something triggered me with the washing machine coins not being the right ones I had and the receptionist not being helpful. It was the straw that broke the camel's back. But the end was very near–only 10 more days. The countdown was on and at least I knew I was done with laundromats. The storm blew over.

We decided to finish the rest of the trip by staying two days in each place. No more moving daily, packing and unpacking. Peace returned to our home on wheels.

The trip did not break us. It brought us closer. Chris even had to cut my fringe every few months as it was impossible to see a hairdresser anywhere without two weeks' notice. There was no escaping each other's idiosyncrasies. We witnessed at close quarters each other's dark side. But we both have a healthy sense of humour. Laughing, dancing and singing saved us. Most of all, our love for each other grew stronger.

We believe firmly after going through that experience together that nothing can faze us now.

CHAPTER 40

Is blood thicker than water?

THEY SAY YOU CAN PICK your friends but not your family. I believe that I picked both. I used to go back regularly to Montreal to visit my family and in particular my parents. As they got older, I went more often, every two years on average. I am the oldest of 5 children and I was guilt-ridden that I was not there to take care of my parents in their golden years. But my brothers and sisters were very supportive and kept a close eye on them.

My father was my favourite parent. My relationship with my mother was not a deeply loving one. However, my mother looked after us the best she could. We never went hungry. We were always well dressed as appearances were important to her. We were cared for in a traditional manner by a stay-at-home mother of the sixties. My mother passed away in December 2020 from a heart attack a year and a half before our trip. It was at the height of COVID. Thankfully, the virtual world we live in now allowed me to attend her funeral via a web camera. We had not spoken to each other for 18 months since my last trip to Montreal. There was so much unfinished business and now that she is gone it will forever remain unfinished...

My father was diagnosed with Alzheimer's Disease in his late seventies. The early signs appeared after he had a few car accidents. He had been driving for decades with a perfect driving record. I don't even know if my father ever had a speeding ticket. But he was losing his driving skills and his memory. My mother was his carer until her death. She possibly suffered from dementia as well. She never wanted to get tested and refused to see doctors in general. The situation at home was untenable, but there was no question they would ever move out of the family home. They had lived there for 60 years. However, there was no choice after her death and my father moved to a nursing home.

I could finally have more contact with him with Skype video calls. Due to his hearing impairment, I had been unable to phone him when he was living at home. He could not hear me. But at the nursing home during COVID, they offered family members contact through Skype calls. I jumped on that opportunity. We had weekly phone calls–something we had never done in all the years I had been in Australia. But it was made even better by being able to see each other. It was so good for the first year and I looked forward to each session. We were reconnecting finally. But I could see each week that he was declining. Eventually, I reduced the calls to fortnightly sessions as he could not recognise me anymore.

A few months before our Big Lap, I decided to go spend one month with him. I organised to travel in March 2022 to Montreal. The borders had just reopened after COVID. I hate winter and the cold, but this was the only time available before our trip. This was not about me; it was about my father and the urgency to see him as soon as I could.

The visit was bittersweet. It was wonderful to spend that time with my dad. I used my occupational therapy skills and knowledge to assess my father's cognitive levels. He declined rapidly in front of my eyes during those four weeks. Even though he did not know who I was, we still had quality time together. Unfortunately, due to COVID restrictions, the first week I could not have my meals with him in the cafeteria. But that limitation was lifted and from the second week we had lunch together in his room. The staff would bring his meal on a tray, and I would have a sandwich. Then in the third week, finally he was allowed to go outside the complex. We took many walks in the local parks. There was a lot of snow, and he could only walk very slowly, but it was enjoyable. My father was always a good walker. I took him to restaurants as they were slowly reopening for dining in. I created some wonderful memories, and I will always treasure that time we had together.

I informed my siblings before I left that I suspected our father did not have much longer on this Earth. I could not tell exactly how much longer of course. But I suspected that by the end of the year he might be gone. I had the saddest of goodbyes with him, hugging him closely. He said, 'Don't cry, don't cry' as I left with my brothers. I knew in my heart I would never see him again. My father died on the 23rd of October 2022. Within two years, I had lost both my parents.

Until it happens, you don't know how much it will hurt. Being at the other end of the world makes it worse. I was feeling the tyranny of distance at a deep level. When you expatriate yourself at the age of 24, you don't think about the repercussions down the track. Certainly, you don't anticipate your parents getting older and dying. You are young, free and enjoying life in Australia. Then it hits you like a tonne of bricks. They have both passed on and life will never be the same.

Grief is a multi-layered experience. It is one grief after another, and they all pile up until it all catches up with you. And weirdly enough it caught up with me on our road trip around Australia. It was very hard for a while and tears would just flow randomly. Set off by a long-forgotten memory, a sign in a museum about a special rosary (my father's name is Rosaire, meaning rosary) or a look-alike person in front of me. Thankfully, I have a very caring husband who hugged me when I needed it.

I had not brought my passport with me and there was no other way I could have been there in person. I was able to attend the funeral via videoconferencing. I was so grateful for modern technology and to be with my siblings in spirit, if not in body.

THE EMOTIONAL JOURNEY

My dad's death was the lowest point in the trip. It is probably the biggest emotional turmoil I will carry for the rest of my life.

Yes, blood is thicker than water.

CHAPTER 41

How does it feel to be back home?

WHEN IT WAS OBVIOUS THAT we were getting close to Queensland again, we talked a lot about how it would be when we got back home. We were not sure how we would fall back into a 'normal life' after almost a year on the road, exploring the great unknown. We anticipated that it may be difficult to adapt to the tedium of daily routine. After all, we had not had two days the same since we had left. We both have a low threshold for boredom. The Big Lap had stimulated our minds and souls beyond expectations. It was surreal to drive up our street and come back to Earth. It felt like we had been tele-transported somewhere alien for 326 days and suddenly dropped back home.

There was the initial excitement of seeing our home again, which appeared much bigger than we remembered. It seems palatial now after living in a 14-square metre space for so long. Yet it is not a big house by today's standards. Everything is relative. We are so pleased to have all that space to move around! The backyard is so pretty and tropical. We always liked the backyard, and it was a major drawcard in buying the house in 2018. But I was looking at it with new eyes: it was greener and more alive. The gardens were overgrown and in need of a good pruning! But that would have to wait.

We realised that we were physically exhausted. Most afternoons on the trip, we would take a nap after stopping for the day at around 4 pm. One hour would suffice to get us back on our feet and ready to go again. We thought it was just retirement kicking in and us showing our age. That routine continued for about two weeks after our return. Then we did not feel we needed it anymore. We had finally restored our energy levels, which had been somewhat depleted in the previous frantic year. What a relief; we were not old after all. We had been running on flat batteries! Hallelujah!

There were all the happy reunions with family and friends. We had missed them, and they had missed us. It is so true that absence makes the heart grow fonder! It also makes me more grateful to be associated one way or another with such lovely people. Our friends are all genuinely nice human beings, and we are so lucky to have them in our lives. You know who you are.

There was more frenetic energy and money spent on fixing the bus and getting it ready for sale. We had to get our other vehicles inspected and registered as we had let everything lapse to save money. We also had to catch up with several medical appointments. There were financial matters to attend to amongst a mountain of letters, one of which was a huge fine from the South Australian police department with many overdue notices. That was stressful.

The tenants had left the house in perfect condition, but we had to get used to where things were and make it our home once again. It took me three weeks to locate the electric toothbrush I had left behind. I did not even remember how to operate my electric floor cleaner or start my motorbike. How easily we forget simple tasks. It is true that if you don't use it, you lose it. Bit by bit we got on top of all the tasks and settled back into our life as we knew it. Then we started reflecting.

You see, we had used the Lap as a reconnaissance trip to look at other suitable places to settle in and I had written a list of them.

There were only seven names on that list. We had strict criteria. It had to be affordable, near the water and relatively small. South Australia was the winner with three places: Perlubie Beach, Streaky Bay and Coffin Bay. Kalbarri (WA) was also a favourite. There could be worse than living in Metung, Victoria. New South Wales has many beautiful spots on the coast, and I would not mind an address in Tathra or Karuah. But after lapping Australia and contemplating if there could be a better place to live, the answer was simply here in Cleveland, Queensland. Sometimes the answer is right in front of your nose. Home is indeed where the heart is, and we have everything we need here.

I hide my light under a bushel, my husband says. I never brag about my academic achievements or the success in my careers. To me they are just the fruit of personal attributes such as an insatiable thirst for knowledge and hard-working ethics, which lead to quick promotions. They are my comfort zones. But the lap of Australia took me out of my comfort zone in a big way. I feel so proud of that epic journey. I still will not be bragging about it as I realise how lucky I was to be able to achieve it. Many trips do not run as smoothly as ours did–luckily.

Now I feel like I cannot stop thinking about the trip. The biggest surprise was this story that was developing in my head–a running commentary on our adventure. It was the beginning of this book. I could not stop it: it was writing itself whether I wanted it or not, mainly at 4 am much to my husband's annoyance! I was processing all that had happened and realising that I had learned a lot. I could not keep it inside of my head and it had to come out. It gave me a purpose to sit down at the computer and just write the story. That was satisfying.

Finally, I had to adapt to not working and that was a brand-new feeling of contentment. I had retired just before the trip started, so I did not know exactly what it would be like to completely be a retiree. The trip was a working holiday no less. I have to say that I am enjoying retirement a lot more than I thought I would. It is early days for sure. I am finally in charge of my destiny, dancing to the beat of my own drum, off the treadmill and all the other cliches you can think of. I worked hard and/or studied relentlessly for 46 years. I either worked full time and studied part time or vice versa–studied full time and worked part time. I did not know anything else until now. The trip was a great transition between two important phases of my life. I do not have 46 years left in me. But whatever is left, I feel blessed to be able to enjoy those years with my nearest and dearest.

There will be more travelling that is for sure. But there will never be another continuous year of travelling. We know that there is so much more to explore, and we will not rest until we have attempted to see it all. Our headstones will not have written on them that we died wondering!

Oh, and remember the neat freak who set out on that trip on the 14th of July? She died sometime in August when it became obvious that she could not win the war against red dirt! It was not a sudden demise. That neat freak just slowly faded away. I had to pick my battles.

In answer to the question, 'How does it feel to be back home?' … In one word: AMAZING!

A FINAL WORD

WE ARE SO GLAD TO have done the Lap, but we are delighted that it is over. I can honestly say now that it is not for everyone. All my friends have said they could never go away for so long. It was a massive endeavour to leave everything and everyone behind for almost one year.

There is a unique way to do the Lap for every traveller. I cannot imagine two vehicles following the exact same route unless they are in a convoy, and we saw a few of those. We met a man who reported driving around Australia in three weeks in his sports car. Of course, he never saw anything but the white line on the road. On the other hand, we met a couple who have been lapping for more than 18 years. They still discover new spots to visit. Australia is so big that you could never live long enough to see it all.

We did a Lap that matched our personalities: a bit keen and erratic! It was partly due to the fact that we were limited to the one-year lease on our house. But we also thrive on surprises. We took to coddiwompling like a fish to water. I don't regret a single thing. I will cherish forever the sweet memories. The bitter memories will be stuffed in the 'experience' drawer of my brain.

My final words of advice: If you feel it in your bones that you need to do a Lap, if you really want to get away from it all, then go for it! Listen to your itchy feet! Unless it is athlete's foot: then go see your doctor.

Prepare as much as you can but eventually you just have to get in that vehicle and drive out of your comfort zone. It is so beautiful out there.

> *"It is good to have an end to journey towards; but it is the journey that matters, in the end."*
> *—Ursula K. Le Guin*

ACKNOWLEDGEMENTS

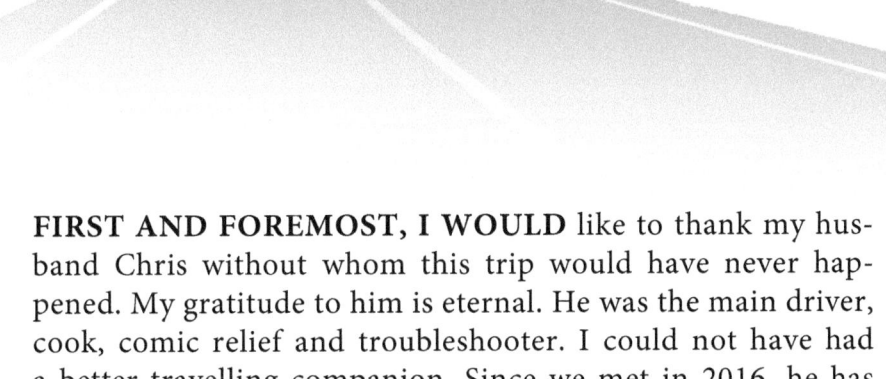

FIRST AND FOREMOST, I WOULD like to thank my husband Chris without whom this trip would have never happened. My gratitude to him is eternal. He was the main driver, cook, comic relief and troubleshooter. I could not have had a better travelling companion. Since we met in 2016, he has made many of my dreams come true. Nothing will ever equal our lap of Australia, but we already have a few ideas for more adventuring together.

I would like to thank my friends who encouraged me to write this book. Some even said from the start that they would buy a copy, which was totally unexpected. A special shout out goes to Geoff K. and Marie France W.

My friend Sharyn was brave enough to read my first draft and provided feedback for which I am very grateful.

After a first pass by Chris, who has edited many theses, the book was perfected by my editor Wendy Millgate-Stuart, and I am so thankful for her way with words. Since English is my second language, her professional input was invaluable. A final proofreading effort was kindly provided by the eagle eyed Pam Tranter and I could not be more appreciative of her assistance.

THE EMOTIONAL JOURNEY

And this book would not exist without Clark and Mackay, book publishing and printing specialists. Jason Smith guided this very green author through the process in the most patient manner. I could not have hoped for a better mentor, and I am indebted to you.

Finally, I would like to mention you, my reader, for joining me on this wild adventure. Writing the book was not a deliberate choice really. I just had to write everything down so I would not forget the trip. It was totally self-indulgent. But you chose to spend time reading and sharing my memories of those extraordinary 326 days. Thank you!

ABOUT THE AUTHOR

MAY B WILD IS FRENCH-CANADIAN and travelled to Sydney in 1985 on a working holiday visa. She fell in love with Australia at first sight and never went back to live in Montreal, becoming an Australian citizen in 1987.

Travelling is one of May's passions. She has journeyed to all continents, including Antarctica.

May has never followed a linear trajectory with anything in her life. Her professional path has had many twists and turns. One of her first careers was as an Officer Cadet with the Canadian Coast Guard. This led to working her way up from deckhand to captain on river cruise ships in Australia. Being an animal lover, it was an easy transition into veterinary nursing for 7 years. It was followed by occupational therapy specialising in mental health for 12 years. It is evident that May has a very curious mind and eclectic interests. She may also suffer from a low threshold for boredom.

Only one thing has been constant–her love of words. Writing poetry and reading have been May's core pastimes since her teenage years. *A Lap of Australia for Beginners* is her first venture in travel writing, brought about through a fascinating journey around mainland Australia in 2022/23.

May lives in Brisbane, Queensland with her two favourite travelling companions: her husband Chris and their dog Watson.

FOR MORE INFORMATION

You will find the stories and photos we could not fit in the book
at the website maybwild.com.au
You can subscribe to the blog to keep up to date.
You can contact the author at maybwild@yahoo.com

UNLEASH YOUR EXPLORER!

www.ingramcontent.com/pod-product-compliance
Lightning Source LLC
Chambersburg PA
CBHW040159100526
44590CB00001B/1